WHAT OTHERS SAY ABOUT
MADELAINE COHEN

"I am one of the lucky people in this world who are fortunate enough to know Madelaine both personally and professionally. She is both strategic and detail-oriented, and always knows inherently what is best for her clients. Madelaine is extremely passionate about health and well-being and practises it in her everyday life, so it is wonderful to see her combine her passion with her business acumen. She is an absolute wonder woman whom I hope you all have the pleasure of working with at some point in your life."

Pip Davis
Director, Group Business Development ANZ at Collinson Group

"As a business woman, I utilise all manners of social media daily; what I do not do is issue recommendations for those who I cannot speak with certainty and experience of. With Madelaine, it is a pleasure to say that if you are savvy enough to engage her expertise and services, you have added a significant benefit to your circle of business excellence. Madelaine can talk the talk and walk the walk; she has years of proven business results in all financial climates to validate her formulas for success. Madelaine listens, engages and supports people in a calm and caring manner and easily builds trust and rapport. I highly recommend Madelaine as a train the trainer expert and general business advisor."

Helen Treloar
Leadership Developmentalist - Coach Mentor Trainer Confidante

The
Lateral-Thinking
ENTREPRENEUR

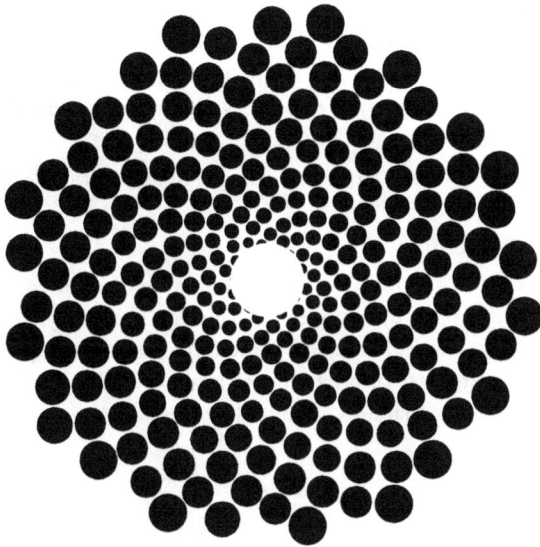

33 Strategies To Transform
Your Business Success

Madelaine Cohen

Premium Wellness
PUBLISHING

DISCLAIMER

The information contained within this book is strictly for educational purposes and is for general comment only. If you wish to apply ideas contained in this book, you are taking full responsibility for your actions. The author has made every effort to ensure the accuracy of the information within this book was correct at time of publication. The author does not assume and hereby disclaims any liability to any party for any loss, damage, or disruption caused by errors or omissions, whether such errors or omissions result from accident, negligence, or any other cause. It is recommended that the reader obtain their own independent advice.

All references to Chirofamily Chirosports in this book are solely in relation to the author's business located in Coogee, New South Wales, Australia which is independently owned and operated. Chirofamily Chirosports and the author make no representations in relation to any of the other independently owned businesses also bearing the Chirosports name.

Names and identifying details have been changed to protect the identity of individuals.

Cover Design and Formatting: Tash Lewin

Edited by: Julie Lewin

National Library of Australia

Cataloguing-in-Publication entry:

Cohen, Madelaine, 1971-

The Lateral-Thinking Entrepreneur: 33 Strategies To Transform Your Business Success

1st Edition

ISBN: 978-0-9953926-8

1. Entrepreneur 2. Leadership 3. Strategies 4. Career 5. Business

Also by the Author: The Lateral-Thinking Entrepreneur: 33 Principles for Expansive Leadership

Published by Premium Wellness Publishing

PO Box 1686, Bondi Junction NSW 1355 Australia

Email: madelaine@madelainecohen.com

Phone: + 61 2 9211 8153

DEDICATION

To my team at Chirofamily Chirosports in Coogee
you inspire me everyday

To those who have the courage to be a leader
I am grateful for the impact you make
to the world we live in

ACKNOWLEDGEMENTS

When I was a teenager my first mentor in business was herself a young entrepreneur. She was my manager at a fashion retail store. One day I wanted to take initiative with something I was working on and she asked me why I was hesitating. I told her I did not want to step on anyone else's toes. She suggested to me that I instead "squish" the toes of the other person. She meant well and was trying to help me and it felt uncomfortable. I knew I would find an even better way to bring out the best in myself and others and to work collaboratively, inspire and be a part of leading people to success in positive ways. I knew intuitively that leadership is lateral thinking. Her advice to me was a positive, priceless gift in defining the business person I am today.

I would like to thank my brothers Daniel, Antony, Nicholas and my sister Natasha for their unique entrepreneurship. I find your incredible careers a source of immense pride and inspiration. We have brought 10 children into the world plus one more soon to arrive so she will make 11 and as they now become the unique free spirited souls just like us, I can hardly wait to see what the next generation of Moulis' will contribute to the world.

Thank you to my mother Nicki and late father Theo for immigrating to Australia and for your personal success in the lucky country. I will always have gratitude for the hard work you both did for your children without any hesitation, question or complaint.

Thank you to my staff at Chirofamily Chirosports, in Sydney's Eastern suburbs. Your aptitude in human connection and your willingness to serve the community is something I am very proud of. You provide me with the means to be able to test my theories and then have a fabulous sense of humour when the learning continues.

To my colleague Louise Thurgood-Phillips with whom I sit on a Board in the not-for-profit sector, thank you for your collaboration and robust discussion. The poignant moments we have shared making some tough decisions and correcting course over many years will never be erased as some of the finest moments I have witnessed in leadership.

To our amazing clients who are so deeply connected to being a part of our heart space. I love it that you argue about who has been cared for by us for the longest. I love your stories about the years we have helped you transform your lives. You are the reason we do what we do.

Thank you to my business mentor and the editor of my books Julie Lewin. Your honesty and integrity is incredible.

To Mac and Indiana, you are two of the most incredible humans on the planet and I am so grateful you chose me to be your mother. You are so funny, delightful and capable. And to my partner Michael Jeffreys, thank you for your encouragement and your belief in me. What you see in me is what I see in you.

CONTENTS

PREFACE

Do you want to love every moment of being a respected leader while you successfully create the most amazing business imaginable in the service industry? You can do this and even more, in far less time and with far less effort than you ever imagined when you think laterally.

For the last 25 years, I have reverse-engineered and taken a lateral thinking approach to creating step-by-step business success strategies. These strategies have enabled me to love my work and help other business owners and professionals thrive beyond their highest expectations. They have also brought love and connection into the lives of thousands of clients, patients and customers because of the generous leadership shown by the business success stories who have followed my strategies.

In this book, I show you 33 amazing step-by-step business success strategies that until now were only available to my mentoring clients. It's time for you to step into a new level of leadership for the purpose of accelerating your abundant success. As a companion to my book, "The Lateral Thinking Entrepreneur - 33 Principles for Expansive Leadership" you now also have a 'how to' guide of strategies that work with the lateral thinking of entrepreneurship.

The choice is always yours. There's no secret in this though: success comes with doing the work. May every step you take have a momentum that is quantum in the direction of your dreams? As I always know to be true; the high road is never easy and yet it is infinitely more rewarding than living a life of quiet desperation.

Thank you for the immense difference you make to the life of one human soul at a time. As a business leader in the service industry you are about to appreciate, and maybe for the first time, the depth of meaning in the smallest things you do. Create a resonance of generosity around all that you are, and attract your business success like never before.

As you take your unique gift to the world I am grateful that, just like me, you are willing to be responsible for service to others.

When you look at the ocean in the sunlight what do you see? Whatever you see is absolutely right, as is what the next person sees. When I look at the ocean in the sunlight I see a billion diamonds. Look for what makes you happy in all aspects of your business. What do you see?

My wish is to meet you one day and to hear about your journey to business success and all the facets that make it amazing.

With love & gratitude,

Madelaine Cohen

Entrepreneur / Business Mentor / Author

INTRODUCTION

Deciding to "retire" from employment at the age of twenty-one was probably one of the most exhilarating days of my life. For the last 25 years I have been successfully living my self-titled retirement as a marketing and personal communication consultant and a business owner.

I was born in Canberra, the fourth child of five and a first generation Australian to Greek parents. My mother arrived in Australia by seaplane at age 6 and my father by ship at age 16. Always entrepreneurs, my memories of childhood involved my parent's long working hours with a pause at 3 in the afternoon to collect us from school. As a restaurateur my father started work by 8 in the morning until well after midnight six days a week. He was an extremely generous man with a love of people and communication. This passion came through in everything he created.

By age ten, I was eagerly spending my Saturday afternoons following my father around in one of his restaurants, cafes or snack bar. Barely able to see over the high counter I became great at making a milkshake and filling bags of cinnamon doughnuts. I learnt how to treat customers often through extraordinary embarrassment as his staff would so excitedly tower over me eager to teach the bosses kids how to look after customers. I loved it and I learnt so much from these weekends as a child.

My experience in observing my father in his business taught me you can make something from seemingly nothing and you can be the most exceptionally skilled person in your field, but if you want to truly succeed at the highest level you must be an outstanding people person and communicator.

My father was obsessed with the New South Wales Higher School Certificate (HSC), for graduating final year high school students, but, in Canberra the only school in the 1980's offering this certification was Canberra Boys Grammar. This meant if you were a girl you sat the Australian Capital Territory Leaving Certificate something my father believed was second rate. Working hard to put five children through a private school education, my father and mother decided to send my twin sister and me to Kambala in Sydney to finish our high school years so we could sit what he deemed to be the "all important" ticket to career success, the HSC.

I was grateful from the moment I started living in Sydney. Now more than 30 years on, I am blessed by the opportunities that were available to me. At 16, I started working as a sales assistant for the clothing retailer Country Road and continued to work in fashion retail until I was 21. I decided to start a University degree and quickly became bored, later deciding after several years of study I just didn't need it.

As National Retail Manager of a chain of retail stores at just 21, the day came when I decided I would be in my own business and that this would be my last pay cheque from an employer.

That day was superb, but as the reality set in during the days, weeks, months and early years that followed my steep learning curve taught me how to be a dynamic business person like I never imagined possible. The lessons I learnt were at times tragic and embarrassing. I was able to learn about the good and bad in everyone, the pitfalls of seemingly good advice, when to stop flogging a proverbial dead horse, and ultimately how to be a business success.

I spent fifteen years in Sports Marketing as a consultant in the Marketing Departments of Olympic, Asian and Commonwealth Games and bringing about the strategies, marketing and leverage needed to earn my clients tens of millions of dollars from a blank page with a deadline of between 2 and 4 years. To do this, I employed a team of outstanding expert consultants who I then seconded into the offices of my clients. I also took a one man Chiropractor working alone in a small medical practice and showed him how to create a brand, duplicate himself and create a business that employs experts who duplicate his success.

Today, I am the owner of this Chiropractic business and yes, I'm not a Chiropractor. I also mentor business owners, small businesses, medium enterprises and multi-national corporations and show how to bring the best out of yourself and the people around you. I sit as non-Executive Director and Vice-President on a Board in the not-for-profit sector. And I mentor Consultants, Healthcare Professionals, Hairdressers, Chiropractors, Physiotherapists, Massage Therapists, Acupuncturists, Beauty Therapists, Bookkeepers, Accountants, Technicians and many other small business owners in the service industry who trade time for income and are looking to grow with ease and achieve the business success of their dreams. I am an author and keynote speaker. And I am a single parent to two gorgeous children.

Everything I share with you in this book is designed to expedite your success. I have now been an entrepreneur and in my self-titled "retirement" for twenty-five years. My life lessons in business started thirty-five years ago behind the counter making milkshakes and donuts. Following the ideas and inspiration I share with you is for more than your financial and business success. Your lifestyle and your love for what you want will be magnified to a whole new dimension when you live in a place of ease and grace by simplifying and focussing on what I know to be the most important keys to your success.

I suggest you use this book as a companion in your business. Focus on the areas you most want to shift and change. Apply the practical steps to achieve the outcome, be consistent and watch the magic happen as you transform your life even more.

CHAPTER 1:
LEADERSHIP

It all starts and ends with leadership. How you live and embody leadership when you trade your time for income as a professional or consultant in business is one of the most important determinants of your success. We are all energy and our communication is only 7% words. People feel your presence before you open your mouth. When your state of physiology is in leader mode clients will pick up on this immediately. Most of the time, I believe they don't even need to hear your voice to know you are the expert they can trust. When you see yourself as a leader the world responds in remarkable ways.

In this chapter, I share two transformational stories where professionals I have mentored embraced leadership with remarkable results and I show you how to be the leader in your field.

One day I was mentoring Katherine, a Chiropractor. She was concerned that after seeing her new clients for just a few visits they typically fell out of care never to return. She was feeling invisible and was concerned that her income was heading in a downward spiral. Her work days felt draining and hard. On a Monday morning her schedule was showing a patchy week at best. When she saw a new client booking in her schedule she started to feel a sense of dread. Given that I was on the end of the phone and couldn't see her, I asked Katherine if she was seated or standing. She told me she was seated. In my conversation with her I noticed her quiet, dejected tone of voice and asked her to describe how she was sitting and how her body felt. Just listening to her tone of voice I could feel she was shrugged, hunched and bent forward. I had this vision of her all curled up and wanting to hide. This was pretty much how she described herself. With her soft and meek voice she sounded like she had lost her self-confidence. I talked through how she conducted her initial consultation with a new client and then how she planned their care. It became really obvious to me that Katherine wasn't being a leader for her clients from the outset, or at any stage of their care. As a result, they lost confidence in her within a few short appointments. In her physiology alone, she was unable to give her new clients a sense that she was the expert leader who could help them. Katherine's presentation to the world was showing up as invisible. What I mean by this is she displayed such a lack of self-confidence that her clients couldn't connect with her.

Leadership starts with physiology and a feeling of esteem and self-confidence. When you model the typical poise of a leader, their feet are firmly planted on the ground, shoulders are back, lungs are open and their voice is clear and confident. When you are in the business of being a consultant or professional providing personal services and you deal one-on-one with a client, you must display leadership in your engagement and interaction. Your client is paying you for advice, assistance or a service. They have come to you to engage your skills and expertise. Your role is to lead your client to the successful outcome they are paying you for.

Mentoring Katherine on this day reminded me of a time when I was training a group of five Chiropractors. This training session was a turning point in my understanding of the invisible person. One of the Chiropractors in the group was so absent I literally kept forgetting she was in the room. I approached her after the session and did some exercises one on one with her to help her stand in her physiology of leadership and everything about her changed in minutes. Her skin tone became brighter, her posture taller, her voice changed completely and she was back in her body firmly. She was standing tall and proud. She felt completely different. Luckily for Katherine, I had the step by step resources to help her regain her confidence as a leader. I will share this with you soon.

Jim is a Physiotherapist who had been in private practice for two years when he started business mentoring sessions with me. He decided to specialise in sports injuries. In his first mentoring session, Jim was unsure as to whether I could help him. He felt his big problem was a skills issue and maybe he just needed more training in the field of science and physiotherapy technique. Jim's problem was his perceived inability to get results with his clients. He lost his confidence because he felt clients were not recovering and moving past their injuries.

We started at the beginning. I asked Jim to tell me about his consultation structure with clients and to talk me through what he says to them. Within a few minutes, I realised that Jim had the technical "know how" and what he was missing was the ability to lead his client to the health and recovery outcome they needed. His vague filtering of words to protect a feeling he may be rejected was costing his clients valuable recovery delays. Jim knew what to say and do and was weak in sharing this with his clients. He preferred to leave them with a barely competent understanding of the process and what they needed to do in partnership with him to influence their recovery.

This experience is relatively commonplace. Jim's desire to "please people" meant he lacked the assertiveness he needed for them to respect and follow his guidance and leadership. Instead of being thoroughly direct in a caring manner, Jim left his clients with little direct guidance and poor leadership which meant that between consultations home therapy recommendations were not being followed. Jim's wishy washy approach meant his clients were being left to decide when they should seek more care. Consequently, his lack of leadership meant his clients were missing out on results. His technical knowledge was brilliant. He simply failed to be a leader. After he embodied leadership qualities, Jim's results were quite remarkable.

Leadership is defined as the ability to cause a person to go with you by holding their hand. It is initiative in action and you make yourself an example for others to follow. It's about showing the way and leading in advance. It involves stepping into mastery, governance and clear direction. Physiology is defined as the study of normal function in living systems. In psychology, it is defined as the study of nervous system mechanisms in perception and behaviour. In other words, the physiology of leadership means your ability to see, hear, feel and become aware through your senses and behaviour the actions you need to do and the person you need to be in order to take people in a clear direction.

In your consulting business, your leadership helps you retain clients and achieve the outcomes your clients want and pay you for. It helps you to be energised and self-confident. It gives you the best opportunity for excellence in your earning capacity. It also takes you away from losing clients. It helps you ensure your good reputation is upheld, encourages people to refer other people to you and say good things about how you helped them.

Some theorists believe leaders are born and also made. My feeling is that if you decide to be in a career or business that involves people coming to you for advice, physical treatment or you are an independent service provider, your ability to embody leadership is essential to your success. Leadership is a choice. Every leader in history was at one stage given the opportunity to say "yes!" They may have been encouraged by others and ultimately made the decision to lead. Even if you've had the best training, education and opportunities, if you decide to be hidden in the crowd, you can never lead.

When I think about leadership the qualities that come to mind are dependable, integrity, inspirational, visionary, encouraging, positive, charismatic, confident, builds confidence in others, dynamic, decisive, intelligent, articulate, problem solver and great communicator. I also feel leaders have high emotional intelligence and behavioural flexibility.

The following activities can help you lead:

Before you start every work day embody the physiology of leadership in your physical being.

- Stand comfortably tall with your feet planted firmly on the ground.

- Get a sense that you are truly connected to the earth below.

- Open your airway by putting your shoulders back and opening your chest and throat area.

- Open your throat by relaxing your neck muscles.

- Relax your shoulders from your ears and allow your arms to hang comfortably by your side.

- Look straight ahead and then soften your gaze to get a sense of the space around you, to the left, the right and behind you.

- Engage a subtle sense of peripheral vision.

- Now close your eyes softly.

- Take three deep breaths. In through your nose and out through your mouth.

- Get a sense of what it feels like to have the intelligence of the universe pouring into your head and down through your body.

- See this as a rainbow light that fills you and the space around you.

- As you do this tune into direction, confidence, decisiveness and taking the lead.

- How does it feel to be a leader? What do you look like? How do people see you? What do you say? Your tone of voice is strong, dependable, commanding and caring.

- Feel or get a sense of what it feels like to be able to deal amazingly with every situation you are going to meet today. What are you going to say to your clients? How are you going to inspire and direct them? What actions are you going to require them to take as a consequence of your advice and your leadership? Feel what it feels like when you truly help people, to guide them, to make them feel safe and secure, for them to know they can depend on you. What level of honesty are you embodying right now?

Create your own leadership affirmation. I have created many of these over time and I say them aloud every day, especially before working with clients.

My favourite leadership affirmation is this one:

*"I am of service. Everything I want and need
comes to me easily and effortlessly now. I share my
strength, humour, leadership, honesty and knowledge
– whatever it takes – to help the people I work with
today and every day to achieve the life of their
dreams."*

Set the environment before you work with any client. If you are in an office or they come to your premises, create an environment you are in control of. It needs to be organised, professional and representative of who you are and how you lead. If you are on the phone, be in the right space to focus on your client. Turn off distractions and push notifications. Be in a space that says you are working, focussed and on task.

If you want to be a leader you have to have control of the consultation process from the beginning to the end. This means you don't feel it out, you actually take control. Give clear and decisive instructions and wait until they are followed. What too many people do in this situation is they wait to find out what people want. This is second base. First base is to make sure your client knows you are in control. If clients don't follow your directions from the beginning, they won't follow them down the track either. Now, this isn't about pushing your client. Be who you are, be the person from whom they seek knowledge, and in this be congruent all the way. The way you express yourself will give you a response which you need to listen for. A client who feels bullied will shy away. When you take control, it is with care and firm kindness that leads your client to get results.

Always show flow in your process with your clients. Have a system and framework that you follow with clients. This consistency allows your client to feel led to the outcome. Within this you will need flexibility. If you are a healthcare practitioner and every appointment starts with a few questions, some physical examinations, a short discussion about care and then the care itself – be consistent with your order. If you are an advisor, create an appointment structure for all meetings. Take your clients on a journey, this tells their non-conscious you are their leader.

Look for commitments from your client as you work with them. I learnt this from attending many Tony Robbins seminars over the years. He makes having his audience, "say yes!" an art form. When I mentor clients, I want positive commitment throughout the consultation. I ask questions I know they will answer with, "yes!" I ask them is this, "good or good?" I want my clients to give me positive reinforcement throughout and with this I know that I am influencing their results by making sure they are 100% committed to what is possible.

Have absolute belief in what you are doing. You are a beacon of energy. Even the puppy walking down the street can feel the energy of a person who is scared. Your belief that you are amazing at what you do and that you deliver outstanding results and value for every client you work with is paramount to your leadership success.

Always show enthusiasm. The best leaders who inspire others to greatness keep their vibrational energy high and are enthusiastic. The boring, mopey, shy, dry and complaining people are not who you want to be around. Bright and enthusiastic energy engages and inspires people. Be infectious with your enthusiasm. Your clients will follow your lead and will want to be around you.

My client Jim realised his lack of self-confidence to lead his clients in their treatment protocols, both in clinic and at home was the problem. He shifted his physiology into leadership and within a matter of weeks his compliance levels improved more than 70% and his clients suddenly got the results he thought needed more technical skills.

Katherine the Chiropractor used the physiology of leadership exercise, created an affirmation, used "yes" commitments in consultations and took the lead. Within three weeks, Katherine had grown by an additional 20 client visits per week.

In consulting and service based work, your ability to lead is one of the most important determinants of your success. In every transaction with a client, when you lead you take them on a journey and when they lead you are left dealing with limitations.

CHAPTER 2
BUSINESS HOURS

When you trade your time for income your business hours are more important than you may realise in helping you succeed. I frequently hear from tired and burnt our practitioners, consultants and service based business owners who are exhausted by their work. I find planning business hours an important step to alleviate this issue. When you master the action steps to determine what your business hours need to be to maximise your hourly rate, you may find these simple actions create magical results for business growth, too. This may seem counter intuitive. It's a lateral approach to improve your efficiency and create an energising effect on what you do. For most people, their goal is achieved by reducing hours and working smarter instead of longer.

In this chapter, I show you how to plan and structure your business hours; business management time; scheduling and marketing time to increase your personal energy levels, effectiveness and business success.

I started working with Lynn a hairdresser in a busy city location when she had become burnt out from working long hours. Many of my clients work in service based industries and healthcare where physical, mental and emotional exertion are all heavily involved in a day at work. You typically stand up and do physical work, while needing to be mentally alert. At the same time, you often deal with the emotional presentation from your clients. In healthcare, it's pain, stress and physical illness. As I pointed out to my hairdresser client in her mentoring session, you cut off a part of people's past. Many hairdressers I meet are street smart "virtual psychologists" who deal with the emotional baggage their clients express while having a haircut.

Lynn was feeling burnt out from long hours. She was forced to work at lunchtime because her city location meant this was a popular time and her early mornings and evenings were always full. The challenge for her was that when she had a gap she'd just spend more time with the client ahead of it and in the end she was working 48 hours a week cutting hair in the salon alone. After work, she needed to look after her accounts and stay ahead of marketing.

I got excited when I looked at Lynn's appointment schedule. I could see how tired she was and I also saw an amazing opportunity for her to increase her income and reduce her work hours. You see Lynn had some classic traits in her appointment book that were making her work for much longer than she needed to.

When you trade your time for income the efficiency of your business hours is paramount to your success. You may charge a per hour fee and when you extrapolate this across a long working week of saggy time and stretching out client consultations you discover you are earning far less than you imagined. This means you have little free time and your quality of life is impacted.

Setting your business hours as a consultant needs to be based on efficiency and the pace you set needs to ensure you are always energised and motivated. When you work with people as a service provider and leader you need to keep your vibrational energy high so you are just as focussed and on task at all times of the day from early to late.

Your hours are designed to maximise your income, your efficiency, keep you in a high energy state and maximise your free recreational time. So avoid long days and don't drag appointments out longer than needed just because you have a gap and want to avoid becoming drained.

When you schedule your business hours correctly, the chances of physical injury, tiredness, brain fatigue and burnout are less likely to occur. If you plan a long career in your field, it is an essential choice you need to make for your health and wellbeing. Approximately 1 in 5 business bankruptcies in Australia is attributed to ill health.

These are the ideas I suggest for your schedule and to get your business hours right.

Decide on your services and exactly how long each service takes. Make sure you are really clear on this. It's a busy world and your client's value when you are on time for their appointment. If you have different types of appointments determine the length of each.

Work out the most energy lifting times of the day that work for you in business. You may prefer mornings, like school hours, afternoons, evenings or anytime. It's your choice. As an entrepreneur in the service industry and a specialist in your field, you need to be in control of the work hours that mean you are always at your best for your clients.

Take into consideration the peak times for your clients. For example, if you are a hairdresser in a CBD area there may be extra demand early in the morning, at lunchtime or in the evening. Other locations have different peak times. I mentor a fitness instructor who is busy from 6 am until 10 am and then from 4 pm to 8 pm. You need to know your market and your location and choose the peak times.

Next I divide a whole day into 3 shifts. For most consultants, working to a 3 shift business hours schedule is a great solution. In my Chiropractic clinic in Sydney, we have 7.30 am to 11 am (followed by a 30-minute break or exchange of practitioner), 11.30 am to 3 pm (followed by a 30-minute break or exchange of practitioner) and then 3.30 pm to 7.30 pm. Some days, a practitioner will do two shifts with a short break, sometimes they will do 2 shifts with a long break of the entire middle shift and some days they will just do one short shift. Given that I also want to optimise the use of space in the clinic, as happens in many shared workspaces, this scheduling means I can make the best use of time keeping all the consulting rooms occupied. In addition to healthcare, this same principle is also excellent for businesses like beauty therapy and hairdressing where maximising client scheduling efficiency and return per square metre of space is important.

If you have long appointments and shorter ones, work out if it is best to offer certain services during certain times only. In many healthcare modalities, an initial consultation has a very different flow and energy requirement to a standard treatment consultation. It can be effective to select certain times when you are best energised and equipped in your mindset as the leader to have longer consultations.

Now you need to be absolutely honest and look back over at least 3-6 months of your business schedule and work out your average number of consultations by type per week. You are about to radically reassess your working hours by consolidating to create some scarcity and give yourself a much more focussed work week. You will also give yourself free time by cutting out the "waiting for clients" time and the gaps between appointments.

Your task now is to create business hours that better reflect the number of hours required to serve your clients with minimal gaps. Try to set shifts using the 3 per day suggestion rather than a few hours here and there or long days with no breaks. As you grow you can add shifts. Many consultants are challenged to take regular breaks and the truth is that having a break is essential for your short, medium and long term health and wellbeing. To be at your highest vibration, focussed, alert and energised you need to stop even for just 30 minutes get some fresh water, fresh air, fresh food and a fresh perspective.

Now you need to cluster book your clients. No gaps. Trust in your ability to use your time efficiently with clients and book them in clusters. By cluster, I mean group them one after the other. When a client wants to schedule an appointment you lead them to the times that best work for your cluster bookings. You are the leader responsible for giving them the best of you, and so you need to decide the best time to see your client. You choose, not them.

It never ceases to amaze me how when a consultant or specialist in the service industry who is in high demand has a waiting list, no matter how inconvenient the time, if the client truly wants to see them they make the time work for when the specialist consultant can see them. By tightening your business hours you create the same pressure on your schedule as that of a highly sought after specialist with a waitlist. The energy that goes with you being in control of the most efficient business hours creates a new magic. You might see the demand on your time suddenly becomes greater and the respect that clients have for you based on perceived scarcity of hours is incredible.

As your time fills and you create a wait list, you can then open a new session. Only do this one session at a time because your aim is to consolidate your work hours, maximise your hourly earning rate and have some well-deserved and amazing free time to truly enjoy yourself.

My mentoring clients who use this strategy maintain and grow their income. In fact the income growth is almost instantaneous. The extra time they have means time to run their administration, accounts and marketing without interruption. In addition, having some free time for lifestyle balance such as exercise and personal time has an incredibly positive flow on impact into the energy and vibration of your working time, too.

Lynn the hairdresser ended up cutting her business hours in half when she first reorganised her appointment book to increase her efficiency and her hourly rate. She ended up having a full day off every Monday. Something she had not achieved in her working career. As the first few months progressed of her new business hours she told her clients her hours had changed and this resulted in them becoming eager to pre-book their appointments well in advance as they were concerned they may miss out or end up on a waiting list for an appointment. Her hours did increase again, in a measured way to meet demand, and she maintained control of placing clients into her schedule at the times that meant she worked with all of her energy and at a high vibration. Her earnings have gone up by nearly 25%, her true hourly rate remains high and she is happier and healthier than she has been in years.

Taking steps to have business hours that maximise your income and your free time is an essential aspect of your business success.

CHAPTER 3
CLIENT MOTIVATION

Seeking to understand your client is essential for developing a long term business relationship that makes them feel valued and gives them the best opportunity for a positive experience. Many years ago, I listened really carefully to the advice about when it comes to the non-conscious mind your gatekeeper has a proverbial "stop sign" when someone says to you, "I understand." I tried this theory on by being vigilant with listening to my inner self when I heard these words. Over many months, I experimented with my internal dialogue when someone made the statement, "I understand." Interesting, most of the time, the voice in my head said, "How could you possibly understand? You're not me!" I observed that when someone claimed to understand, my internal defences popped up time and time again.

I changed my words and changed my world.

This experience led me to ask people if they could "help me to understand" and the results in my human interaction were astounding. I gained an experience of having other people really open up to giving me the information I needed to be of service to them. In this chapter, I share with you the gift of seeking to understand your clients by asking them to help you to understand them even better. The initial key to appreciating the motivation of your client is to make it clear to them that you have a willingness to understand them, and, in order to get it right you will need their help.

The more you are able to appreciate how your client behaves and operates in the world the better you will be able to work with their model of the world. With this insight you will gain a vital window to what motivates them.

In discovering your client's motivation, this helps you to have an understanding of the concept of "logical levels above" in the process of being able to identify where your client is functioning within the process of change and communication. In Neuro Linguistic Programming this concept is identified as a natural hierarchy. Cultural anthropologist Gregory Bateson suggested that making changes at an upper level in the hierarchy would change everything below it to support the higher level of change. I often talk about taking the high road, maintaining a high vibration and staying logical levels above because as the leader rises and maintains a high level of leadership physiology, expansive awareness and the qualities of spirituality in terms of knowing and staying true to purpose, the natural tendency is that whatever is operating at a lower level will also rise. The term "be the change you want to see in others" is embodied in the concept of being logical levels above.

In the hierarchy of logical levels the lowest level is environment. The emphasis is 'where' to change. Above environment is behaviour and in this 'what' to change. Next are capabilities and skills defining 'how' to change? Above this are values and beliefs asking 'why' make change? The second highest level is identity where you ask does the change reflect 'who' I am? At the top of the natural hierarchy of change is spirituality defining the 'purpose' of change.

When working with clients to discover their motivation having appreciation for the logical levels above hierarchy of change enables you to position your influence at the highest levels, in order to elicit an upward movement in the propensity for your client to achieve results. I refer to this concept as working at logical levels above. The advantages of this include being able to maintain a high vibrational frequency keeping your energy levels high and enabling you to stay above drama that may be evident at lower levels of logic.

The first step to this process is to simply observe the presentation when you meet them. If you see your clients in an office, clinic, store, salon or public environment this will be easier than if you are working with them by phone. It can be helpful to offer a new client a session by Skype or Facetime so you can "meet them face to face" and see them at least once when you start working with them. These days though you can often find images of your clients on the internet and through social media and these will give you a good idea about how they present themselves to the world.

The purpose of visual observation is to gauge their visual appreciation of themselves. This has little to do with economics. I've met people who earn a mediocre wage and yet dress impeccably even opting for fine handmade Italian suits with their focus being on quality and appearance instead of quantity and a one season wardrobe. People who take pride in their physical appearance tend to be visual processors meaning they learn in pictures. They will often use visual related words like "see" and "look." You may find a visual person moves quickly and talks quickly. The first key to understanding them is to appreciate how something looks matters to them. These clients will be looking at the state of your office from a visual perspective. When you work with a visual client they appreciate everything looking good and they like speed.

In an absolute dichotomy, one day I went to the office of an Optometrist and it was visually unappealing. He asked me to assist him with his business as a mentor. The office was chaotic, and at first, I found this intriguing as I sought to understand the client. I had an uninformed preconception that being a vision specialist that the office would be great on the eye – visually appealing! How wrong I was. Then the practitioner emerged slowly from his office and I mean slowly. He took little pride in his appearance and spoke very slowly. In his hands, he held what appeared to be a cotton thread that he was fidgeting with. This practitioner was kinesthetic meaning he was a feeling person. For a kinesthetic client to feel understood, the focus needs to be on how they are feeling. The pace of interaction with them needs to be slower and checking in with them will always be about ensuring they feel right.

An auditory processing client will tend to use language related to listening, speaking, hearing, tone and the like. These clients will want you to hear them. They tend to operate at a medium pace and when you are communicating you will want to check in to ensure everything you are saying or doing sounds right to them.

The auditory-digital client will tend to want process in their interactions with you on the basis of facts. This person is typically analytical. When you have a client who is an auditory-digital processor their methods will be about facts and statistics. They tend to be working in professions that require a high level of analytical skill. As a stereotype, many accountants are auditory digital processors.

Once you have observed your clients and listened to their verbal cues, make a few notes on whether you have observed them to be a preferred visual, auditory, kinesthetic or auditory-digital processor. I often will ask someone some questions when I think I have worked it out.

Here are some of the questions I suggest:

"So do you think you might be a visual person, meaning you like things to look good and get the most out of being around people who are fast? Do you have a *picture* of what I'm getting at? Am I *seeing* this right?"

"I'm intuiting that you really need to be *heard*. *Tell* me, how important is it that you have people around who actively *listen* to you? Does this *sound* correct?"

"Does that *feel* right? Can you give me a *sense* of whether we are on track?

"How does that *add up* for you? Does that *compute* in your mind?

Step two is to ask questions that enable you to appreciate another person's thinking. There can be no right or wrong when you understand that there are so many factors that go into a person's impression of a situation and the world they live in.

I often use the enquiry, "Can you help me to understand?" to make sure I am respecting and eliciting all of the information I need in order to help someone.

Step three is to listen for keywords and key phrases and then repeat these back to your client. Many people use the same words and phrases repeatedly and feeding these back to your clients helps them to feel understood.

As basic as it may seem, step four is to use your client's name frequently. People love hearing their own name and making a point of using someone's name is a great way to help them feel understood.

My optometrist client wanted to grow his business, and to do this, I first needed to assess exactly where his strengths and weaknesses in business lay. By seeking to understand his model of the world, I was able to set the right pace to lead him to the success he was looking for. It became an exciting journey because by first working out the gaps and continually ensuring I truly understood him the changes he was able to implement came from a place of authenticity and trust. He made remarkable changes to his business and through learning about human behaviour in the process he was able to observe his clients, assess their presentation and help them based on a new level of understanding. He now always acts as a leader in his business.

Leadership is a place of calm when you realise your role is to seek to understand another human being before you use their model of the world to take them on a journey to the outcomes they seek. Observation is the key. When you ask the right questions and make sure you use their specific language this is life changing for your client and your success.

CHAPTER 4
HOW TO ASSERT YOUR CREDIBILITY

In this chapter, I show you how to become the expert and how to establish your credibility with all of your clients. The most important thing about establishing your credibility is that people are aware you are truly accomplished in your field, experienced, and that you know your facts.

The majority of people who are the right market for your services and expertise will only come to you if they feel you are extremely knowledgeable in your profession and that you truly know what you are talking about and what you are doing. Consumers today have an incredible amount of choice and so your ability to differentiate your services through a professional and thorough approach to asserting your credibility makes a difference to your success.

So many practitioners and business people I work with hide their facts from other people thinking it's boastful or they won't be appreciated for sharing all the information they have stored in their brain.

The truth is that the exact opposite is needed.

One day, I was working with a medical doctor called Robert. He had an absolutely insatiable appetite for learning. He would read all the time, and he spent a lot of time researching the things that interested him.

What I found very interesting about Robert is that he did not share any of this information. He didn't share it with his clients, and he didn't share it with his colleagues. He just kept it to himself. He actually thought that it was egotistical to share this information with people and that people would think he was big-noting himself.

One day, he was asked to speak at a local medical group that had an audience of doctors and patients. The night was organised by the local government health network and professionals from the area had been invited to speak to the group on different topics in relation to health. He was very nervous, but he decided to go and do the talk.

At the end of the talk, someone who knew him really well came up to him and said, "Robert, I am absolutely amazed. I had no idea you were such a specialist in your field and that you have such an incredible level of knowledge."

Robert was gobsmacked. He had no idea himself that someone would be so interested in what he had learnt. This taught Robert an incredible lesson about the importance of making himself accessible and open to sharing his expert knowledge. He realised a personal cost of avoiding this was impacting his business success. After thinking about this, Robert also felt he was far more energised when he was sharing the knowledge he was storing in his mind.

Why is it important for you to establish your credibility and allow people to understand how much knowledge you have in your field? The first reason is that you want to be considered a specialist in your field. A specialist will always be the person of choice in competitive industries.

Set yourself apart from everybody else in your profession. This shows you are really good at what you do. If you want other people to refer to you, you need to be giving them a high level of knowledge.

Almost 25% of people will only work with or go to professionals who they believe know their facts. The only thing they are ready to listen to when they walk into your office or connect with you is the facts you can share with them that will make them know they are in the right place.

By sharing this information, you increase the value you bring to your clients, and overall this is really important for how you set your pricing. People who feel they are dealing with somebody knowledgeable are more likely to refer other people to that person. This results in increased bookings, increased income, and an increased level of influence for you in your profession. Not sharing your knowledge means you are going to fall into the pitfalls of being average.

If you set out to not share what you know on the basis that you feel it is boastful or it's unprofessional for you to be sharing everything you have learned, then you're just going to be average. That's no way to run a business.

Here are some ideas for you to use your knowledge and credentials in a way that is ethical, credible, and practical:

- Read, learn, and give facts to your clients. Make a point to learn new information relevant to your profession every week.

- Give people dates, times, and statistics. I find this is the best way to give short bits of information that really shows you have knowledge in your field.

- Put your credentials on your wall so when a client comes

into your office to see you, they know immediately you are a professional in your field and you have the knowledge and the understanding of what you share with them.

- As you attend different courses, get a certificate for those courses and add them to your credentials on the wall. You want to make sure your office is filled with certificates that show you are someone who has knowledge.

- Share the information you discover by creating a weekly fact sheet. Keep this nearby in your office as a reminder, and use these facts for the week or month. What you want to do is keep the information very short and simple, and at the same time very informative and relevant to your industry and clients.

- Join groups on LinkedIn and other websites that help you to work and collaborate with professionals in your field and learn from them. Discover what they are interested in, and what they are teaching their clients. Then research these subjects as well so you can understand what the most important developments are in your industry. If there's a certain topic that interests you or there are certain cases and themes coming up in the work you do with your clients, do some extra research into this.

- Go onto the Internet and find information that gives facts, figures, and statistics about what it is you need to know more of. Then share this with your clients.

- Watch TED Talks. This is a terrific way to increase your knowledge. While these talks may not always be auditory, digital, and analytical, often they provide a very interesting understanding of human behaviour and some really great facts you can share with your clients. The most important thing to do is to share and be deliberate about how you do this.

Back to my client Robert, the doctor. He embraced the fact he was a learner and decided to share this with his clients every day in his practice. As a consequence, his new client referrals increased dramatically. In fact, over a three month period, they doubled.

He now considers himself to have specialist status. This is reflected in the number of clients who re-book their next appointments at the time of consultation and feel they can approach him and ask questions they would otherwise not have asked him in the past.

What Robert realised was that, in order to set himself apart, it was not boastful for him to share all the information and knowledge he had in his field of work.

Willingness to share knowledge is a very important part of developing your business and helping your business to grow.

CHAPTER 5
SETTING OUT THE STEPS

You may have been working with somebody for a very long time. It's not uncommon for healthcare practitioners, bookkeepers and hairdressers, for example, to have the same clients for 10 or more years. Yet, with that client, are you taking them on a journey, or are you just leaving them stuck where they were when they first came in?

Do you ever get a sense when you're working with somebody over a long period of time that you completely lose track of where you're up to with them? When you take your clients on a journey it makes your work so much easier. In business, I frequently hear about the cost of retaining clients. Over the years I've kept a keen eye on assessing the circumstances that lead to clients being retained and the circumstances that lead to them dropping out. In this chapter, I share with you the secrets of retaining clients by taking them on a journey.

I think all consulting and all service based businesses need to look at setting out the steps of a specific journey to go on with every client, and that you need to make sure you stay on track in following a process.

A number of years ago, I was contacted by a naturopath who needed some help with her business and she was keen for my help. Being a naturopath, she said her business was very complex and often cases came with a lot of different issues which required her help in order to get the client well again, and then take them on a pathway to health.

She found that no sooner had she started working with people and they would actually drop out of care. She felt she wasn't being given the right amount of time in order to get them the first set of results that would help them on their journey to health.

I sat with her and discussed the programs she gives to her clients, and how she explained it to them. What I realised was she actually lacked a plan for how she was going to help every client, and therefore, she wasn't taking her clients on a journey, and they were getting lost in the process.

Becoming lost in the process was perhaps making the clients feel they weren't getting results from her care, which may or may not have been correct. The bottom line is that without her giving her clients any benchmarks or predictions and neglecting to keep their expectations managed in a systematic way, her clients didn't know whether they were actually getting what they had paid for or not.

The naturopath was very frustrated by this situation, and found the effort she put into her clients very early in their care was being met with rejection as they dropped out. Thankfully, I had a solution for her.

A journey is simply the process of taking your client from point A to point B.

Nearly 20 percent of people want to know how something works in a step by step manner. They want to know the process. They want to try it out and do it, but they also need to know what steps are involved. They tend to start with an idea. They need things to be usable so they know how it works. They like to know what the theory is behind something, and they need to be shown this with a common sense approach. These people like to be coached and facilitated, and they actually make outstanding clients when you understand how they think. The benefits of this are many. It creates long-term clients. It helps you to get results. It makes you very thorough in your work. When you set out a process and take your clients on a journey you end up setting a high standard of professionalism and you can more easily avoid missing something in your client's care or in the work you do for your client. You can avoid doing half a job and more than ever, you can avoid a client leaving after the very beginning, and falling out of care, or falling out of service with you before you would like that to happen.

There are a number of steps you can take that show people what you're going to do with them, and how your system of consulting to them will actually work. It doesn't matter what industry you're in. You could be in healthcare. You could be in some other form of business consulting. You could be in hairdressing. You could be in any service business, and this formula still works.

Step 1 - Initial Consultation

Start with a step by step formal initial consultation appointment. In that initial consultation, you're going to get some background information. You're going to create a rapport with your client, and find out what they like, and what they don't like. Be sure to take lots of notes on what that is.

Most importantly, you're going to find out in that consultation what your client wants and you're also going to explain to them what you feel they need.

Step 2 - Testing

The next step is to actually undertake some tests. I know that may seem illogical for some businesses. You need to appreciate there's always a testing process that is involved in you actually doing a good job for your client. There's no business where you as the leader and professional is exempt from making an assessment of your client based on your knowledge and expertise. Your client has come to you for the fact that you know more than they do, otherwise, they would not require your services. It's your role to investigate behind a face and words to ensure you are using your skills to deliver a result.

A weight loss client may want to lose 30 kg and when you do your tests you may find they have a health issue that was hidden from view and needs to be addressed before weight loss can start. It may be that your client would like to go from a brunette to a blonde, but when you actually test the quality in the fibre of their hair, you realise that's going to be difficult. If you're a healthcare practitioner, then there are lots of different tests you will do. Medical doctors run tests. Naturopaths may look at live blood analysis, blood tests, heavy metal toxicity screenings, etc. A chiropractor will look at the nervous system and do neurological testing, balance testing, posture analysis, and maybe order some X-rays for the client. In business, you need to find out what's happened in the past and then match this with current circumstances and factor in where that person really wants to go. Then set the journey.

In step 2 you undertake a thorough analysis.

Step 3 - Program Phases

The next step is to set out some program phases of how you're going to work with your client. The best way to do this is to divide it into three different phases.

In the first phase, you're going to deal with exactly what they want to achieve as the presenting situation. Exactly what they would like to have as the first step is always going to depend on the analysis you have predicted for them, and the answers they have come up with in terms of where they would like to go. Sometimes your client will not get to their outcome immediately, and that needs to be set out.

The first process you need to undertake with them in your program phase number one is to recognize where the client is at and move them past that first phase of what they're trying to achieve. At the end of this phase, it's really important to give the client a re-assessment, to actually sit down and have a discussion about where they're at and whether they're happy with the results. You can then do some further analysis and testing with them to make sure they're achieving, or on the process of achieving, what they set out to do with you.

Phase two becomes a consolidation phase. It doesn't matter what industry you're in. It's really important to have a consolidation phase with your client.

Sometimes, when a client comes to you for a service based consulting solution; you'll find the next step they need to take is to be in a position where they understand the changes they've made will take a certain amount of repetition and changing habits in order for them to maintain what's been achieved.

In the second phase, I always look at this as consolidation, whether it's in healthcare, social services, or it's in business, the next phase is always about consolidating what you've accomplished in phase one.

When you feel as though that accomplishment has been achieved, and the consolidation has happened, the routine is in place, and the new habits are there, then the third phase is to move on to what we call more of a well-being phase.

In healthcare, well-being makes sense. Even in other industries, well-being also makes sense. If you just help somebody in their business to make some big changes, then you want to be able to maintain the well-being of that business by checking in as a consultant with your client frequently.

For example, if you've just created and gone through the phase of helping somebody grow their hair, and now they have their beautiful new hairstyle, you want to be able to maintain that and help them to look fantastic going forward. That's going to take a level of maintenance care.

If you're working with somebody on their health, and they've now achieved the level of health that you predicted they might get to with the efforts they've put in, in phase one and phase two, you now want to maintain those efforts by having regular appointments with them and making sure they stay on track.

This is a journey. It starts with an initial consultation and takes clients all the way to their outcome, and beyond their outcome; which is that you become an important part of their life by helping them to stay on track. By setting out these steps from the beginning, this helps your client have a predictable understanding of what they're going to go through with you.

By re-assessing your client at least three times along the way before you get to the stage where you are just working with them from the point of view of maintenance, or what I call a well-being program. You are actually helping them to understand that changes will not happen overnight and it will take time. That time will involve commitment to your services and a commitment to the steps you've set out for them.

You'll know very quickly with a new client, whether they want to do this or not. It would be so much better for you to have an understanding from them, at the very beginning, that they're not interested in a high level of care and support from you. Remember as the leader you set the program of how you'd like to work with your clients. For business success, I suggest you keep it systematic.

If they are in, then you just need to make sure that you keep reminding them of the journey they're on with you, and as you go through each step you let them know which step they're up to. This is a terrific way to not only get results with your client, but to actually take them on a journey. If a client is out, then you'll know very quickly and the best solution is to always let them find their way with someone else. To maintain a high level of success and keep your energetic vibration high in business you need to be discerning and know when to release a client who is misaligned with your offer and the journey you take your clients on.

Back to my naturopath – she did have a system she used for all of her clients. The challenge was she wasn't telling them. There was nothing written or nothing spoken about the process she was going to take with every client. We created a presentation for her that she could give to every client on their initial consultation, and we also discussed how she should conduct a progress review in order to make sure she reminded clients of the journey and the steps she was taking them on. This enabled her clients to have a really good understanding of where it was they were at, and where they were going with their health. She ended up keeping clients in care and getting far better results. More importantly, she ended up having clients who stayed well into the well-being phase, because they understood the process and had been educated along the way. As a consequence of this, she grew her business significantly and became a lot more confident as a practitioner, understanding that her clients simply needed to know the journey they were going on from the beginning, in order to achieve the results they wanted in the end.

This is a really important phase of you being a terrific leader in your consulting or your service industry business. What are the steps you take with every client? Are you telling them you're taking these steps, or are you keeping it a secret?

It's important you allow your clients to appreciate that the changes they want, whether it be in business, health, or lifestyle choices, will take time, and that your method of working with them is to take them on a journey. Lay out the steps for them, so you make this easy, and make sure you help them along the way by doing a really good review of the stage they're up to. This can be transformative for your business.

CHAPTER 6
VIP SERVICE

Business these days is really competitive, and I get a sense this competitiveness makes it not easy for clients to decipher who the best service provider is for their needs. I hear all the time that practitioners find it challenging and small business people find it hard to retain clients. What I see is it is the small things that aren't being done that may make a world of difference.

In this chapter, I show you the easiest ways for you to roll out the red carpet. When you roll out the red carpet you give people a level of service they are not expecting. Everyone wants to be treated as a VIP, and there are many simple, easy ways in which you can do this in your business to make your clients feel very special.

Why would you want to do this? The most important reason why you do this is because people want to be cared for. Today, most people live in very big cities where, even though they are around a lot of people, it can be lonely and life can be disconnected. The level of connection you can offer people is important to them in terms of how it helps them live a better life.

People want to be cared for. They want to be noticed. When it comes down to it, it's often the small things that people remember, good or bad, about your service that will be their lasting impression of you.

If you want to create long term great business relationships with your clients, the best thing you can do is to wow them with red-carpet service, and it's much easier than you imagine.

I want to share a story with you about my own practice. As you may know, I am not a chiropractor, and I own a very successful chiropractic practice in Sydney. The business has been established for more than 20 years, and in this time, I have really enjoyed the fact that I have been able to work with incredible professionals. At the moment, I have six full time chiropractors working in my practice. They provide exceptional service to our community, and I am very proud of what they do.

One of the things we do in our practice is we offer our red-carpet service. This is the level of service people are not expecting, and it comes with some very interesting stories when you realise the impact this has on other people.

Recently, one of my chiropractic assistants was speaking to a client in reception and the client had a very important business pitch they were doing in the next couple of days for a client overseas. The explanation was this client had to wake up early in the morning, put on a suit, get onto Skype, and speak to their client across the world in order to see if they could put together the best possible outcome to get the deal.

The client was very nervous about what she was doing and anxious about making sure she got it right, because this was an important time for her in her career.

My chiropractic assistant listened to all of this and made a note in the diary. The day before the pitch was due, she sent a very simple SMS to the client to say, "Hey, I just wanted to let you know that the whole team is behind you and we hope your pitch goes really well. Good luck from your Chirofamily."

This simple message had an incredible impact on our client. Two days later, our client contacted us to say how that message had absolutely changed her confidence and had actually brought her to tears. She said to me not even her own family cared enough to contact her, knowing how important this pitch was.

She felt so pleased that someone she considered to be almost a stranger, a receptionist in our chiropractic clinic, contacted her just to say good luck. She said she told so many people about the amazing experience she had had with us.

On another occasion, one of my chiropractic assistants was listening in to a conversation in reception, and a gentleman was explaining to another client that he was about to go overseas on a long holiday and he was very excited. He had come in for a treatment days before he was due to leave.

My chiropractic assistant made a note in the diary, and, on the day of his departure in the morning, she sent him a very brief SMS message saying, "I know you are leaving today on the holiday of your lifetime, and I just wanted to say have a wonderful time."

A couple of days later, the doctor who looks after this client was walking in the street up at the local shops and from across the street could hear this other man yelling and waving at him madly. The man bolted across the street, across the traffic, and approached the doctor.

He said, "You'll never believe what happened the other day. I was taking my dad to the airport, and he received an SMS from one of your secretaries to say, 'Have an amazing holiday.' I want you to know that my father was absolutely touched by this. He was so happy she had remembered he was going away and she took the time to contact him to say, 'Have an amazing trip.'

This is what I'm referring to as red-carpet service. In my business, we do this every day. These are the things that really matter. Human connection is priceless. In business, you take the high road and you lead. These are the times people really notice you, and, as a consequence, feel they have a special bond with you and your business which is something they don't have elsewhere. Doing this can bring profound outcomes for you as a business person.

I feel red-carpet service in our business has helped us create a very strong referral-based practice in which a lot of people have been with us for many years. In fact, sometimes it can be quite amusing in the reception area listening to clients talking to each other, with some of them actually getting into arguments about how long they have been a client at the practice. Their loyalty is so strong they want the bond to be a lifetime. It can be very entertaining when one person says, "I've definitely been coming for 20 years," and someone says, "Well, I remember when they were in the old location up the road, and I was coming to them back then as well." It's wonderful to have this level of connection with your clients where they feel they belong and they matter.

Here are some ideas on the things you can do and it's very simple to roll out the red carpet for your clients.

- The first thing we do is know our client by name before they come into the practice. When they come into the reception area, we greet them by their name, even if they are a new client, because we are expecting them. We know people like to be called by their first name. On arrival, we always offer them water.

- We select and hand magazines or books to our clients.

- We open doors for our clients whenever we can.

- We always keep only the latest copies of magazines in our practice and make sure that any copy that is more than two months old is recycled.

- We encourage our chiropractic assistants and receptionists to have a chat with clients to find out how they are going in their life.

- When a client is in reception, we check their file and make sure we have completed everything on there. If the client is taking supplements, we ask them how they are going with their prescription and if they need to buy more items.

- At a time when the client is relaxed and still sitting in reception, we offer to put their next appointment in the schedule if it isn't already there. When the doctor is ready to see the patient, we take the client to the room and make sure they are comfortable. We ask them, "Is there anything else that we can get for you?"

- While a client is in their appointment, we offer to look after their children. We play with them and give them the opportunity to come behind the counter and be our helpers.

- We carry babies and look after them so the parents can have some time on their own.

- If a client has lots of items in tow, we offer to carry things to their car for them.

- When it's raining, we have umbrellas and offer to take people to the car or their transport in case it's difficult for them in the wet, and particularly, if they are injured.

- After a consultation, we regularly SMS our clients to see how they are feeling, and we take a genuine interest in the life events that are happening for them.

- If a client tells us about an important event in their life and the timing of it, we make a note and contact them to say we hope it goes well.

- We SMS client appointment reminders to every client 24 hours ahead of their appointment.

- When a practitioner is running late, we phone our client to tell them how many minutes late we are running so we do not inconvenience them.

- If a practitioner is running extremely late, we apologise, and we give our client our coffee voucher so that they can go down the road and have a snack or a coffee while they are waiting.

- When someone is having a birthday, we send them a personalised SMS, not something generic, but something that is really relevant to them.

These are such small things you can do in your business that really make an incredible difference to people's lives.

Rolling out the red carpet and giving VIP service is a very important facet of being the most outstanding business professional in the service industry. If you want to set yourself apart and have clients who tell the world about your business and appreciate what you do for them, use these small steps in order to gain the rapport and the recognition people find most unexpected.

CHAPTER 7
ANTICIPATION

D o you ever feel as though you're standing on eggshells? Have you ever felt stressed when you saw a particular telephone number come up on your telephone handset wondering what the next problem is you're about to answer? I want to open your eyes so you're no longer afraid of what you may see.

A number of years ago, I realised there was a significant amount of power in business by being really good at anticipation. I found by anticipating things, I put my mind at ease, and I was able to get along in business with a far greater level of success. I want to put you at ease and let you know you are not alone.

In my business, I have had a number of situations I haven't antici-pated well. From these, I've had enormous learning curves. In my chiropractic business, I employ associates. When one of these associ-ates leaves the business, there can sometimes be a six or more figure dent in our turnover in a matter of weeks. This can have an incredible impact on the business.

I've observed this in other practices and businesses which hire consultants and people who trade their time for income. When somebody leaves the business, the dent they leave behind can be profound, and can have a significant impact for months and even years.

I'm about to show you how to anticipate in your business so these events no longer impact you. You will get some exceptional results if you look for the signs and know when to anticipate what may happen in the future and be ahead of it and get things right.

The word "anticipate" means to regard something as probable, to expect it, or to predict it, to be prepared. For me, it's about being excited about what's around the corner rather than being stressed about what you might be revealed. This is an important part of anticipation. I use anticipation to motivate me and to find ways in which I can be even better in business while, at the same time, prevent anything from happening that may be detrimental.

When you decide you're going to be excited about anticipation and you look for the opportunity in change, your energy shifts significantly and enables you to move toward your goals even faster.

Sometimes not anticipating things and sticking with the status quo can be quite problematic to your business. It can also be an issue if you get stressed about what might be in the future instead of looking at it as an opportunity for your success.

When you change your mindset around anticipation you ensure what you anticipate is actually good and worthwhile for you. You are more able to embrace change in a positive manner which assists you to move forward proactively.

Why is it important to anticipate what's going to happen in your business? Most importantly, anticipation creates stability. It gives more flow to your business, and this includes cash flow. When you anticipate you are a step ahead of your competition. So many businesses fail to anticipate, and become a part of the status quo of having to deal with lurching from one crisis to another.

Anticipation allows you to stay in a high vibration and allows you to operate above the mundane. Everyone has stories of missed opportunities, and the most important thing you can do is invest in your future.

There's a story I love to share, and it's about a family friend of mine, who, many years ago in South Africa, had a grandfather who was in the horse and cart business. One day, some people came across from the United States and offered this man a partnership in their business which was for Ford motor cars.

The gentleman turned around and said, "Oh, nothing will ever replace the horse and cart. I'm not interested in investing in your business and becoming a partner." Well, of course the horse and cart is no longer our mode of transport, and motor vehicles are! This family tells their "what if" story all the time. To me this is a great example of an instance where a belief system in the value of anticipation could have been an incredible success. Not all great ideas are worth the effort and the foresight to anticipate is the energy here.

What's so interesting is this family continues to tell the story of their grandfather and what might have been had he anticipated that changes in technology would do away with the horse and cart and would mean everyone wanted to drive a motor vehicle.

Here are the top 10 things I feel are very important to anticipate in your business.

1.   The first thing you want to do is invest in your industry. In other words, have a look at what is happening in your industry and the changes to innovation within the industry. By anticipating the

direction your industry is taking, you will find your best source of success.

2.   Look for consumer trends. How is consumer behaviour changing? Look behind the habits of consumers, not just at face value. What are the sorts of things people need? Is it more efficiency, more time, more convenience, a greater use of technology in what you do? These are all the things you need to look for in consumer behaviour, so you are a step ahead of this.

3.   Look at regulations in your industry and how they change. Particularly in the health industry, there are many changes that happen due to regulation. As a consequence of this, if you fail to stay ahead of the regulatory requirements in your industry, you may find you have difficulties in your business. It's important to stay ahead of the regulations and continue to look at changing laws in relation to your industry and in relation to being in business. This includes such things as tax laws, employment laws, and laws that regulate your industry such as regulations on how you practice and how you advertise.

4.   Look at the innovation in your industry and across other industries. There is a lot to be learned through innovation which is designed to save time and money. Anticipate the changes innovation will have on your business, and be ahead of these so you can implement them with ease.

5.   Anticipate staff changes. People will come, and people will go. Unless you pick up the signs when an employee may be ready to leave your organisation or it is time to move an employee on, you will often have challenges in your business. Staff anticipation is the number one thing you need to do if you're employing people in order to be successful. It is important you look for the signs of somebody who might be ready to move on.

6.   Look at technology advancements. How could technology

improve your business? Look at technologies you could implement in your business to create more efficiency in how you run your administration and also create more efficiency in how you deal with your clients.

7. Anticipate competition. Look at the competitors around you and be vigilant in keeping an eye on what is happening in your area which may influence your business. Being aware of competition is an important part of anticipating changes which may occur in your business.

8. Listen to your intuitive thought processes. If you have an inkling about something or something gives you goosebumps, it's time for you to anticipate and look into it. I often find this is a sign you need to take notice of. Your intuitive thought processes and the things that come to you are things you need to listen to. A great part of anticipating and preparing yourself for a great future is to listen to your intuition and listen to it carefully. You are always going to be your best advisor, so if you get a feeling or a sense about something, make sure you follow it up and you follow through.

9. Always anticipate changes to your cash flow. Make sure you have a very good understanding of the ebbs and flows in your business and the impact of seasonal changes. Plan your cash flow accordingly. Many businesses today struggle with stress as a consequence of cash flow and you cannot be failsafe in predicting this may happen to you. In fact, some of the people I mentor have had the most unexpected things happen to their health and there have been major consequences for their business and their families. When you anticipate and have the right sort of insurance in place for your business and your personal protection, you will always be a step ahead of the unexpected. This is vital for you and your success.

10. And finally, when it comes to anticipation, I ask myself every day to look out for the things I need to know in order to be successful.

I put it out there as an energy field. I make sure I look out for the signs that will enable me to prosper in my business, because I realise the importance of anticipation in making sure I am able to work at my best is something I need to be aware of and take very seriously.

When you embrace anticipation, you find it is a very exciting thing to have. It helps you to grow, and it helps you to embrace change. By embracing change you can achieve the goals you want in business.

CHAPTER 8
CHOICE OR DILEMMA?

Thereis much capturing our attention these days, and things move so fast, choices are everywhere. We've got lots of big and small decisions to make every day. Even if you think about it now, if you want to catch a taxi, you have a choice between calling a taxi and calling an Uber. With Uber, you have choices within Uber. You can choose and UberLUX. You can choose an Uber taxi, or you can choose an UberX.

There are many decisions we're forced to make every day through lots of choices. One of the things I feel is really important to understand about consumer behaviour is that people get overloaded by choices. When a choice overloads you, it becomes a dilemma.

When I started my career as a teenager working in retail, there was a sandwich shop down the road from the store I worked at. There were no choices. It was one sandwich shop and only sold sandwiches.

My only choice was which sandwich I wanted to have. I used to

55

contemplate the fact that it was so easy to go there every day and know predictably what I was going to be faced with in terms of a choice for lunch.

Believe it or not, even though that may sound boring, it is much easier on our nervous system and functionality when we have a small number of choices rather than a huge number of choices.

In order to be of service, many providers and service providers I work with want to give their clients lots of choices. The problem with that is when you give people too many choices, it becomes a dilemma, and they make no choice at all. I want to show you what it means to create a business where you give your clients a great number of choices without creating a dilemma.

I was once contacted by a massage therapist who wanted some mentoring help with his business. I had a look at his brochures and his websites. What I found was everything he had on offer gave people far too much choice. He had choices around time. You could have 30 minutes, 45 minutes, 60 minutes, 90 minutes or 120 minutes. He then had a choice of 10 different massage therapies you could buy. I felt this was too much choice. Looking at it as a consumer, I couldn't work out what he was specialising in, what he was really good at, and which choice I should make in terms of deciding what service to take from him.

I spoke to him about the importance of simplifying his business in order to multiply. He liked the fact that he lived an unpredictable life. He liked the fact he had lots of choice, so this was not an easy discussion for me to have with him.

Pretty quickly, he realised that by giving his clients too many choices, and encouraging them within those choices to change their massage therapy style between appointments, caused him problems in his business. He decided to take my advice and simplify the number of options he gave his clients.

Why would you want to do this? It's really important to give people the opportunity to decide between one and another thing. It helps you to be a specialist and for people to understand what it is you're truly good at. You can stabilise and grow your business when you have a very predictable service menu, create a niche, and more importantly than anything, you know you are doing what you love.

Choice is defined as an act of choosing between one or more possibilities. I think the key here is to give people an alternative and an option rather than giving them a whole feast of choices.

A dilemma is defined as a situation in which a difficult choice has to be made between two or more alternatives, especially ones that are equally undesirable or equally desirable. The challenge with it is you end up with a vicious cycle or a mess and a muddle, and a quandary people are unable to get out of.

As a result, you find when people have too many choices and are faced with a dilemma, it becomes a problem for them, and they actually make no choice at all. To avoid people walking away, you need to give them simplified choices.

I had a similar experience working with a personal trainer who had 30, 45, 60, and 90 minute sessions. I said, "Why all the choice? Why don't you just choose one session and make it a 90 minute session or a 60 minute session and say, 'My consulting time is this time only'?" The personal trainer actually followed the advice, and found it was easier to get clients to stay with their programs because he was no longer giving them so much choice.

I learned all about the difference between choice and dilemma when I worked in retail sales in the late 1980's. I worked in a fashion store, and one summer, we ended up with about 20 different styles of white shirt. I realised when a client came in to buy a white shirt, it was very difficult for them to make a choice.

I would look at the client, look at their body shape and get an idea as to what I thought might suit them and look good on them. I only showed them two shirts. Out of the 20, I would say, "Do you like this one or this one?" They would choose one. After they tried it on, if that wasn't right for them, I would only give them two more choices.

I started applying this principle across all my sales in this business. Suddenly, my sales took off in a remarkable manner. I realised, in a store that had more than 250 to 300 choices of items to buy, in terms of narrowing it down to this or that helped my client make a decision much quicker. I was so excited by my discovery I taught my colleagues how to do it, too. We had so much fun being of service to our clients and became more in tune and investigative with them instead of being ad-hoc about our recommendations. We had to do fast client analysis, use our knowledge of the range and match the client to the clothing accurately. Then we limited the choices and helped the clients to make great decisions.

How are you going to apply this to your business?

Firstly, have a look at what all of your services are. In each, you want to be giving people two choices only. How to decide what your best choices are, look at what your current client's most popular choices are then you work out what energises you and what drains you. If there are services you offer as part of your choices which drain you, you need to eliminate them immediately. Replace them with services that energise you. This way, you're giving people the choice between something that makes you feel good all the time.

When you speak to your clients use language which encourages them to choose one or the other. If you have more than one choice, try and predict for the client what the best two choices would be for them, and say, "Would you like this or that?" After you've done that, say nothing, wait, and give your client the opportunity to come back and tell you which choice they would like.

Keep it simple. Always keep your choices very simple and make it very clear what your client will get for each option. This helps your client avoid overwhelm which creates a dilemma and leads to the problem of no choice at all.

You want to be able to multiply your services, and that's where you become a specialist. Make sure you keep it really tight so you do a lot of similar work on a daily basis, but in that you're multiplying what you do and you do it well.

You need to promote your services in very simple and clear ways. Make sure the options are laid out very well and it's easy for a client to see, at a glance, exactly what you do, exactly what they're going to get, and exactly what the two choices or simplified choices are.

What if the client decides to go elsewhere and not to use your services? This not a dilemma at all for you because there are millions of people out there who want what you offer. The important thing is to make sure you always give people choices, and within that, you always do what energises you.

If you provide work that doesn't energise you, there's no point offering it. Your clients won't have the best experience because your energy is not going to be positive while you're working with them. If somebody wants a service you don't provide, send them to a service provider, if you know one, who provides that service and provides it well.

Don't try to be everything to everyone. This creates a dilemma for you, a dilemma for your client, and it drains you in your work.

The most important thing to do is to offer people a choice, let them choose between two things, and then if neither of those choices works for them give them the option to go somewhere else. You're only creating space for the right clients who absolutely want your services by doing this.

CHAPTER 9
REBOOKING YOUR CLIENT

Every client you work with is in until they tell you they're out. What that means is you need to take leadership in making sure you consistently rebook your clients. Make sure they continue to come in and use your services until they turn around and say to you they no longer want to make a booking.

I find in business what is measured really matters. Instead of measuring the final outcome all the time, one of the things I emphasise very strongly in my businesses is to actually measure the action steps that lead to the outcome. One of those action steps I always measure is the rates of rebooking.

In my chiropractic practice, we aim for an 85 percent rebooking rate. What that means is that 85 percent of people who come into the practice today will have a future booking with us. The thing with rebooking clients is you are the leader. You are in control of your client's journey, and so you need to make sure you appropriately rebook your client at the time of consultation.

One day, I was working with a chiropractor who was very overwhelmed. He felt like he was under a tremendous amount of pressure from his assistant. She was getting an enormous amount of phone calls every day and found it very difficult to field the phone calls.

By the time the assistant managed to get through one phone call to rebook a client, the call itself was taking at least three minutes and sometimes longer. On average, from the beginning of the week to the end of the week, his appointments were growing by at least 80-90 bookings.

We worked out if his assistant sat on the phone answering call after call after call, it would take at least four to five solid hours for her to get through those phone calls. Of course, these calls came in over a much longer timeframe so there was little else she could do in the few minutes typically between calls. I felt we could reduce the assistant's phone time for this chiropractor by at least 75 percent, and save her up to eight hours a week of real time which would enable her to do something else.

With the rebooking system I showed my client, he could save a significant amount of time and reduce by up to 75 percent the number of phone calls the practice received from clients needing to rebook an appointment.

Why would you want to do this? First of all, by having efficiency of time, your assistants can spend their time doing other more important things like engaging with people in the business or doing other tasks for you. You can have more predictable weeks. In other words, at the beginning of the week you can know pretty much how the end of the week is going to turn out income-wise and time-wise for you. This will help you be more predictable with your income. When you have income predictability as a consultant, you feel more secure. It also gives you control of the process you're taking your clients on.

The challenge is this. People today are very busy, and as a consequence, are often not in tune with how fast time passes. Unless you are actually defining time and making sure the client has rebooked within the week if that's when they need their next appointment, the chances are they won't see you for several weeks. In fact, if you don't follow them up, they may not see you at all, and then they're off care or and think they no longer require your services. What they'll turn around and say is, "I tried that, but it didn't work."

Many years ago, I was seeing a massage therapist, and I hadn't rescheduled an appointment with him at the time I finished my last massage. Six months later, I received an SMS from him saying I hadn't had a massage in six months. That was the truth! I hadn't had a massage in six months, and I know that having regular treatments like this is really important for my health. I was shocked at how much time had passed. My intention was actually to have a massage once a month, but because I hadn't booked it at the time of my last consultation, and the massage therapist didn't follow me up within one month, six months had passed before I even realised I hadn't had a massage for half a year. Wow. Imagine that. The massage therapist actually missed out on five appointments with me, and I missed out on something that was really important to my health. It doesn't need to be that difficult. I know that getting an 85 percent rebooking rate with your clients is absolutely and completely possible. The reason I know this is because I achieve this in my chiropractic practice.

How are you going to do this? The first thing you need to do is review the chapter on the three-step programs or plans for your clients. This is really important because your clients need to know that they're going on a journey with you, and they need to know what that journey involves.

The key is to schedule complete programs with your clients. In other words, when you start a new plan or a new stage of programming with your client, if it involves a certain number of appointments at a certain distance apart in terms of time, when you give your client that plan, book all of the appointments in one go.

Sometimes you may be booking them for 4, 6, 8, or 10 appointments spaced out along the next period of time, but the most important thing is that those appointments are made. The easiest way to do this for a client is to choose the same time on the same day for them. I find most people like to have a routine for their day's activities. Therefore, if you make it easy by offering a client the same time on the same day for their appointment schedule, you will find they're more likely to turn around and say, "Yes, that works for me."

You also need to be the leader. This is not about asking people if they would like another appointment. It's about using your expertise to make sure you tell them when they need another appointment. They have come to you for your advice, your assistance, or your care. As a result of that, if you are not actually taking the lead and telling your client what they need, or are instead allowing them to decide for themselves, you are not taking them on the journey they have paid you for.

It doesn't matter what you do. You could be a business consultant, a healthcare practitioner, a hairdresser, or any other service person. If you want your clients to go on a journey with you, you need to plan it and you need to pre-book it.

With my hairdresser, I have all of my appointments booked for an entire year at the beginning of every year. The reason for that is I know when my hair needs to be cut and when it needs to be coloured. Therefore, I just book it in on the right day at the right time in order to make it easy for myself. Then I'm not looking at myself in the mirror one day thinking, "Wow. I wonder how long it's been since I've had a haircut." It's all pre-scheduled and this helps me enormously.

I do the same thing with all of my healthcare appointments, and also in my consulting appointments with my business mentors and the people who help me. This way my weeks become very predictable, and I feel as though these things help me to achieve even more in my life.

If your clients do not make future bookings at the time of consultation, either you or your assistant need to contact them and follow them up within a reasonable space of time. Don't wait like the massage therapist for six months when you think you need to see a client every month.

You should be contact them within the month to say, "Hey, you need an appointment now," not wait six months and say to them they haven't been in for such a long time. If you're taking the lead and you know what your client needs, make sure you stand by that and don't wait. You get in touch with them well before the time they actually need your services, and get them to book it in.

Remember, people are always in until they tell you they're out. When you ring up a client or contact them to tell them it's time for their next scheduled appointment on the program you've set out for them, it's completely fine for them to turn around and say, "Hey, I don't want your services," or, "I don't need that appointment right now." That's fine.

What you need to realise is you must take control of how you schedule that client. If they are not following your instructions, that's going to be a part of how you have worked with them and how you have taken them on their journey and educated them, in terms of letting them know exactly what they need.

What if people change their mind and don't want their appointment at the time you've pre-scheduled it? That's fine, be flexible with people. I find most people who have something in their diary will turn up and from time to time people need to change it. That's okay. Don't make anyone feel terrible about that, just be flexible. You will find for the vast majority of people they will turn up for those appointments.

If people are reluctant to go on a program or pre-book appointments, you need to seek to understand why that's happening. For the most part, I think this means you are buying the client's limitations. Limitations simply mean your client is looking for more information to have certainty that what they're doing is actually the right thing and in their best interests. Reluctance means your client needs more information to ascertain this is the right course of care or the right course of consulting they need for their benefit. The limitations associated with this are something you need to seek to understand. This is not about you selling to your client, this is about you eliciting exactly what your client needs in order to make sure you give them what they need, and also what they want.

Back to my chiropractor who was feeling very overwhelmed and his assistant equally overwhelmed by the number of phone calls they were receiving during the week to book clients in. He started taking the approach of being very direct with his clients in putting them on programs.

He also helped them by making sure they left with a rebooking. In fact, pretty quickly he got his rebooking rate up to 90 percent every week. What this means is that 90 percent of his clients were leaving the practice with a forward booking of at least one, but sometimes more than one, and some clients were actually booked in for many months in advance. These actions resulted in a powerful state of putting influence on his clients and making them want to book appointments because sometimes they were missing out on their favourite times. In the end, he had created a waitlist of people. A waitlist for him was not just about being unable to fit in a client at all, but he created it based on the time that client wanted to come in. As a consequence, he had an increased number of bookings from his clients across the board. Within weeks, he had increased his overall numbers for the week by 20-25 client visits. Not only that, he was starting the week at 85 percent and sometimes 90 percent of what he needed in order to finish the week at a high. This completely changed his business. He was far less stressed as was his assistant.

Rebooking your clients on a schedule and taking them on a journey is an amazing tool for a consultant in a service-based business. This is by far one of the strongest tools I have used to grow my businesses. It requires you to be the leader and it requires you to make sure your clients know exactly what journey they're going on with you.

When a client is reluctant, you need to understand you are buying their limitations and they just need more information from you in order to appreciate this is an important part of them getting what they actually need.

When a client is not sure about going on a program or is not sure about rescheduling their appointments, your job is not to sell to them. Your job is to sit down and seek to understand what they need to know in order to appreciate how important this is for them.

This won't happen for everyone, and I can assure you if we can do it for 85 percent of our clients across my business, I'm sure you can do this, too.

CHAPTER 10
CLIENT REVIEWS

Client reviews are a very important part of your consulting business. You need to book them at least two to four times a year with every client.

For a new client, you always need to do a review within the first two to three months. This is a very important part of you keeping your clients on a long term basis and making sure you can keep your energy high when you work with people.

One day, I was working with a bookkeeper. She was working extremely long hours, and she had many of her clients for more than 10 to 15 years, something she was very proud of. But over the years, working with her clients had become very difficult and very draining for her.

The reason for this was there were old habits she accepted from them that she found no longer easy to work with. Her long term clients had not adopted her new systems and modern technology. She found a lot of her work had become inefficient. She knew that efficiency could help her work with more clients and increase her earnings.

There were some clients who would send her a box of tacky, scrunched up receipts and expect her to go through them all. There were others who didn't know when they had to get their information to her by, and sent it days before a tax payment was due. This created problems for her work flow.

She had one client who had payroll on a spreadsheet they sent to her every week that it was littered with mistakes. She would then have to enter it into an accounting program. She found all of this drained her. As a consequence, she worked very long hours and often on weekends.

I knew I could help her with this. We discussed that her arrangements with her clients had become so saggy over the years it was like disintegrating elastic on an old pair of pants that had become extremely loose.

The definition of a review is to assess something formally with the intention of making changes as necessary. The thing is that life in business does not come with an instruction manual.

If you're not going to review things on a regular basis, perhaps the course of action you're taking isn't quite right. It's important to sit down and look at what you're doing and make sure it is the most efficient way of doing things. There's no failure in doing this and changing your course of action. It's only feedback.

Why is this going to help you? It becomes like a client satisfaction survey when you review your clients. It helps you to energise yourself and get rid of things in your work that drain you. It'll increase your efficiency when you do reviews on a regular basis.

You'll get great reinforcement from your clients that everything is OK and they are satisfied with your services. As a consequence of this, a review meeting actually helps you give your clients even greater value for money.

How do you schedule review meetings? Firstly, you need to work out how you will do your review meetings. How often are you going to do them and in what format? What information do you want to get from your client in order to make this effective?

I suggest you create a review interview sheet or appraisal, something you fill in based on how you find working with your client. The best way to do this is to create a list of all the aspects of working with your client that energise you and all the aspects of working with a client that drain you.

You want more of what energises you and makes you efficient and successful in business, so resolve with your clients all the things that drain you. Sometimes this will be up to you and the way you work with them. At other times, it will be a matter of them meeting you halfway and assisting you so you can serve them even better.

I suggest before you have a review meeting with your client you do your own little pre-review. You decide because you're the leader. What's working for you? What's not working for you? What could change? What new technologies, new systems, new planning, and new ideas could you bring into serving them even more?

Is there something you feel would accelerate their progress or make their outcomes of working with you even better? It actually doesn't matter what industry you are in. There are always innovations and things you can do that can change the way you help your clients even more.

When you sit down with your client to have a review meeting, the first thing you need to do is seek to understand. I suggest you ask them some questions and get the information from them first and lead them on a journey, rather than sitting down and letting them know what you've worked out on your own.

This will help you to understand whether they are as aware of what you feel is going on as you think they might be. You can then take a very gentle approach to introducing ideas to them that might help them even more and will make your work with them more efficient and more successful.

When you have finished a review with your client, agree on the changes you're going to make and implement them ASAP. This may also mean you put them on a program where you're going to schedule all of their appointments with you. Or simply change the way in which you communicate with them and receive information.

Sometimes clients need to be told where things aren't working for you in terms of benefiting them. As soon as they're advised of this, they can change that straight away. Most of the time, they have no idea, so it's a great to sit down and give them some feedback.

Back to my bookkeeper. She sat down with each of her clients and thought about all the things that drained her and energised her in working with them. Some really interesting themes came up. She sat down with each client, most of whom she had been working with for 10 to 15 years, and performed an "efficiency review" of their work.

They loved these meetings. They found them extremely productive and motivating. They also helped because they were being introduced to new technologies that previously they hadn't thought of. This was going to make their work so much easier and more accurate.

As a consequence of these increased efficiencies, my bookkeeper was much happier. She ended up being able to reduce her work hours considerably due to the new efficiencies and she was able to create some space for new clients.

By looking at the list of what drained her and what energised her, she was able to determine in advance the things she would look for in her new clients. This gave her the confidence to choose clients who had the right ingredients so she could be super-efficient for them and do a great job. And at the same time keep her energy high.

Client reviews are an essential part of your business in the service industry. They keep your energy high. It's important to sit down and look at what drains you; have the courage to discuss this with your clients; and have a really honest look at how to make things better. The outcome is that everyone wins because everyone gets heard.

Over years of working with clients, I find that lots of things change. It's important to sit down and keep redefining what the goals are and redefining the ways in which you're going to do this. It can be amazing when you have clients for a very long period of time, but when your relationship with them has become saggy elastic, that can be very draining.

Doing a review on a regular basis with long term clients at least twice a year or more can create an amazing outcome for your business.

CHAPTER 11
REFERRAL MOMENTS

A lot of people I work with seem to feel uncomfortable about asking for referrals. I hear this all the time and what I see are opportunities that are important to act on.

One day I was at a conference and I was talking to a doctor. He told me about how he received lots of praise for all the amazing work he did. I said, "How do you feel about this when people praise you?"

He said to me, "I just feel embarrassed and sometimes I go really red." I thought, "Isn't that interesting?" I said, "How busy are you at the moment?" He said, "Well, that's interesting, too." Because he said, "I actually think that people think that I'm a lot busier than I really am. I hear people all the time saying, 'Oh, he must be really, really busy,' but actually I'm not and that bothers me."

I had some great ideas for him and I was really happy that this had come up.

Referrals are very important for your business. A referral is to make mention of or to introduce somebody. It's really important to make this a feature of your marketing every day. To have somebody introduce somebody else to your business is the best form of advertising. It enables you to work with the type of people you like, increase your income, and you can dedicate quality time to marketing every day in a very simple way.

There are a few very easy ways in order to get more referrals.

First of all, when a new client contacts you, the first thing I always ask that client is this. "Who can I thank for referring you?" It may sound like a really weird question and sometimes they'll say, "Google," or sometimes they will say, "I read about you," or "Somebody told me about you," but the most important thing is that you've put out there right from the beginning that you are a referral based business.

This brings me to my second point. Make sure that all of your clients know you are a referral based business and that you are taking on new clients. Don't make the assumption they will just refer to you without making sure they know you run your business by referrals.

If you have a website, put on your website that you are a referral-based business so people understand that's part of how you market yourself. If you have an office, put signs up in your office that say, "Thank you for your referrals," so people understand that's an important part of what you do.

Most importantly, look for peak referral moments with your clients. A peak referral moment is any moment that somebody gives you praise for what you've done. There are some really terrific ways in which you can respond to this immediately. In all businesses, a lot of people will say at the end of an appointment, "Wow, thank you. You've really helped me." It's a great opportunity to take that as a peak referral moment and to say to that client, "You know what? It's been a pleasure helping you and I love working with people just like you. If you have friends and family who also need my help, please feel free to refer them to me." By speaking to somebody when they're in a peak referral moment and they're giving you positive feedback, they're more likely to take that on board and actually go out there and see if other people need your help.

The same things happen with your assistants, if you have a receptionist or somebody looking after your bookings. If clients say to that person, "Wow, that was amazing," or "I really appreciated the service today," make sure that your assistants know to turn around and say, "You know what? That's wonderful because we really like looking after you, and it would be wonderful to have your friends and family come in, too. Only, if they're just like you though!!" You are edifying your client at the same time as encouraging a referral.

Then welcome those referred people into your practice or into your business by making sure you acknowledge the person they have been referred by.

Another thing you can do is create specialist moments in the times where you look after certain specific problems or cases that interest you. I use this often in my business where someone will say to me that they have a certain issue going on in their business.

After I've helped them solve it, I will say to them this, "You know what? I really like looking after the problem you've come in with. If you know other business people who also have this problem in their business, I would really like to help them with that, so please feel free to refer them to me."

Another idea to get more referrals is to tell your clients you have great news. Tell them you've changed your business hours or added new hours on and you have the ability to take new clients. Invite them to refer new clients! This is a terrific way of getting more referrals.

What if you ask for referrals and you still don't get them? Asking for referrals is actually more of an energy thing than just the words you use. It's actually saying to the universe, "Hey, I'm open to receive. I'm open to bring more people in. I'm open to have more clients."

Some of your clients will refer and some of them won't refer and that's not the point. The point is unless you're putting the energy out there to say, "I welcome referrals," nobody is going to know you want to increase your business.

Back to my doctor. He really took advantage of all the ideas I shared with him. He contacted me within a couple of months to tell me his average of new clients had increased by six per week. He was absolutely thrilled with this result and he was doing no other form of marketing to grow his business. The only thing he was doing was putting it out there that he was open to receiving referrals.

This is a terrific tool for you to use in your business to grow and to make sure that your clients know you like working with people who are just like them, and you're willing to welcome them into your business.

CHAPTER 12
CROSS INDUSTRY REFERRALS

T his is by far one of my most favourite reverse engineers. I think very laterally about cross industry referrals and I want to share some terrific ideas with you that will change the way you think about asking other professionals to refer other clients to you.

So often I look at marketing programs that emphasise having people write letters to other professionals to ask them to refer clients. I find this really troubling. Why would somebody refer to you, when they have no idea who you are and very little idea of your reputation and what you've achieved? I know I certainly wouldn't refer to you unless I knew something about you. I am a huge referrer to other professionals and I take extremely seriously the outcome every person achieves from a recommendation I've made. The quality of their experience is a reflection on me.

So often in business, I find consultants and small business owners send a plethora of letters asking for referrals to different people who they feel might refer to them. Here's the problem, these letters land on someone's desk and the person receiving it has no idea of who you are and no reason to refer to you in the first place.

I'm going to change all of that for you and create the most amazing solution for you to get cross industry referrals. I'm going to share with you the complete opposite of what most people do.

When it comes to cross industry referrals, I believe you need to give in order to get. Here's my strategy.

What I suggest is you first choose the professionals who you most want to deal with and you start looking for opportunities to refer your clients to them.

The reason why you want to do this is because it puts you in the position of professional and specialist in your field and it shows other professionals you are expansive and collaborative in how you do business. They want to know you are generous.

The thing that works amazingly well with this is as a consultant and professional in your field, you might be like a lot of other people out there who find it very easy to give and extremely difficult to receive. So often I deal with professionals, consultants, healthcare people, and business people who are so good at giving and when it comes to receiving they find this isn't easy.

Imagine that you find somebody you most want to do business with and who you feel has a clientele you can also offer your services to. I'm talking about complementary services here. Perhaps you're working in the healthcare industry and you see a fitness instructor you feel may have clients that have sports injuries, or injuries you could take care of. They would be a good person for you to work with.

Or perhaps you're in the health industry and there's a medical specialist you feel might be able to offer services you can't offer your clients. This would also be someone you could work with. Or say, for instance, you consult in another area, e.g., you could be a beautician and you know a hairdresser down the road who has a very similar clientele to you, but you can offer that clientele a different service to what the hairdresser is offering them.

This is what I mean about finding complementary service providers you want to work with. This is how you're going to get their attention. You start referring to them well before you ask them to refer to you. What happens is you start to create a rapport with that person without even meeting them.

In the medical profession, I've had a very interesting example of this with a chiropractor who wanted to create a relationship with a local GP. What he did was this: Whenever he had a case that he felt needed the assistance of a general practitioner, he would pick up the phone and ring that GP's office.

In a very official voice he would say who he was and that he wanted to speak to the doctor in order to be able to refer a patient to that doctor for immediate care. He did this over several months, contacting the doctor several times with clients who he knew needed the care of a GP and didn't have one to go to.

At first, the receptionist was very reluctant to let the calls go through, but within a short space of time she knew it was important those calls go straight through to the doctor so the case could be discussed. The chiropractor was getting on the phone with the doctor and having very interesting discussions about what he thought of the patient's outcomes, and then sending them straight to the doctor who was giving them VIP service. The GP's secretary became so accustomed to the phone calls, she put them through to the doctor mid-consultation and he always picked up the phone to speak to the chiropractor. He knew the chiropractor wanted to speak about another case he was about to refer to the GP and this was something the GP started to find extremely interesting.

Then one day a most amazing thing happened. The doctor picked up the phone and rang the chiropractor and said to the chiropractor, "I have a patient here who I think you can help." They discussed the case and the doctor sent the patient straight down to the chiropractor's office and the chiropractor was able to help that patient.

Immediately on seeing that patient and putting them onto a care program, the chiropractor wrote back to the doctor and picked up the phone to tell him what the case was going to entail.

As a consequence of that, they started to share many client cases and, in fact, rang each other almost weekly with different cases they could share between their practices. The rapport they created was amazing. This happened because the chiropractor started by referring. He knew the secret of getting referrals and that is you have to give in order to get.

How are you going to do this? What are you going to do in order to get referrals from other practitioners? The first thing you're going to do is you're going to choose your top four to six people you feel could most refer to you and you feel you could refer to. You're simply going to look for moments where you can contact that person to refer somebody you know for their assistance.

In that time you can also create a rapport with that person. If you find over a short period of time they're not receptive, you simply find somebody else.

The next thing you're going to do is put yourself in the position of being an equal specialist. So often I find when a business person or practitioner is looking for a referral they put themselves into a position of weakness as though they're begging for business. Nobody is going to refer to somebody if they don't think that person is an absolute professional and at the top of their field.

Before you even pick up the phone or contact somebody for a referral or in that frame of mind to refer to them, make sure you consider yourself to be an equal specialist in your field to the person you're contacting. There's no point contacting them out of a position of weakness and out of a position of begging because as human energy goes, they will pick that up and feel it in an instant. It's not going to serve you.

The next thing you need to do is know how to "pull rank." To pull rank means to use the power of position to get something you want. The secret here is you must view yourself as a leader to do this. If you feel you are inferior then you are simply not ready to have a professional rapport with another specialist. I know that because you are reading this book. You are standing in your magnificence as a professional and you are ready to be at the top of your field. This means being able to have the confidence to pick up the phone and ring somebody and have a conversation with them in order to be able to refer them somebody you feel needs their help.

This is really important. You don't want to be weak about this. You want to be strong. Your whole business is about helping people and about making sure they get the help they need. If you can't do that, the most important thing you can do is to actually help them by sending them to a person who can.

Back to my doctor. My doctor has an incredible referral based business now. This chiropractor and doctor have created the most amazing formula they have both duplicated in order to get the referrals they need to let their business thrive by working with professionals who have complementary services to what they offer.

This is by far the most successful way to get referrals. Not only that, it keeps you esteemed as you do it. It doesn't make you feel like you're begging for anyone's assistance. It makes you feel as though you're a professional who is doing the right thing by your clients. That's how a referral should be from another professional.

This is a terrific way in which you can create even greater marketing for yourself in a very easy way that means you are looked upon as a specialist in your field.

CHAPTER 13
STICK TO YOUR GUNS

There's something remarkable in Arthur Cohn's quote, "You have to believe, you have to stick to your guns." I've heard this quote so many times. Sometimes I have a vision of standing tall, ready for any combative situation in business, with my resources ready to go into action. Other times, I have a vision of super-glue and a weapon, as a type of imaginary protection field. I want the challenges of business to stay away so if the energy is that I have personal weaponry at the ready I am all good. Super-glue is great for permanent solutions. Most times to me sticking to my guns has meant being vigilant to personalities that are misaligned with my goals and my direction.

In this chapter, I share with you how to be observant of some negative subtle personality types who may be a challenge for you in business and career; how to test if your association with a person or group is still good for you; and to know when the time is right to be outstanding at saying "no" and goodbye to people who are no longer appropriate for your business success journey.

I first became interested in this subject when my late father said to me, "See this bucket of water? What happens when I put my arm in it? And what happens when I pull my arm out again? Where's the hole from where my arm was?" I was fascinated, there is no "hole" I told him because the water filled the space. He then told me, "This is what happens when you say goodbye to people you no longer want in your business, there's no hole left when they go." I love it when people talk about the proverbial 'smoking hole in the earth' in the context of what you fear may happen when a person makes brave and dynamic changes. I'm yet to see it.

In business, I make it a priority to look for personality subtleties I feel pose a challenge in my business and be fast at removing the draining people who, while they may have been of service and good at one stage, are no longer relevant.

I have become so attuned to this that recently when I was in the process of offering a person a job in one of my businesses I was called to listen to my intuition. The interview process was going well and we made an employment offer. The candidate responded to the offer re-questing a higher commencement salary. My PA and I looked at the correspondence from the candidate and decided to tune into what may have been going on. We asked ourselves, "What might someone believe to respond in this way?" I was open to paying more, and yet intuitive-ly I knew I was going to withdraw the offer entirely for a very specific and counter-intuitive reason. My PA and I asked the candidate for 24 hours to consider the response. The next day my PA and I met. We had both come to the same conclusion. A subtlety we saw in the per-sonality of the candidate was our answer. It was hidden in plain view. The candidate was thinking about remuneration yes and we agreed this was important. We were willing to pay a little more for the right person. But the right person was someone who would show cause and give reasons for being worth a higher salary, show some excitement for the role and make us feel equally engaged in the contribution they would bring to the business to seal the deal. I was so relieved to have a step-by-step approach to assessing personality subtlety that guided me to withdraw the offer and avoid a lot of potential heartache.

Sticking to your guns is defined as refusal to change your beliefs or actions. Personality subtleties are defined as a part of someone's behaviour that may not be easy to notice. This makes it hard to distinguish within the combination of characteristics that form an individual's distinctive character. Saying "no" and letting people go by being direct in your actions is defined as k-no-wing intuitively, testing with a step-by-step process and taking the signs seriously enough that you are prepared to give the other person the gift of freedom while you make space for someone who is aligned with and can better deliver your success outcome.

So why is sticking to your guns, assessing personality subtleties and becoming outstanding at letting the wrong people go so important?

Your freedom to succeed unhindered is engraved in your ability to have the courage to master these actions. The right people around you help you thrive massively. They create positive energy and their appreciation is immense. The wrong people drain you, they hinder your success and they hold you back. This can come at a massive cost.

Here are the steps to sticking to your guns:

1. Define your not-negotiables. These are going to be your red flags. When one of these is tested, you know you are being put on notice to stick to your guns.

2. Know your plan and be tuned in to how others follow it. Off plan signs that emerge need instant attention. If they are remedied with ease then great, if not look for subtleties in personality.

3. Have an accountability buddy. Someone outside your business whom you trust to show you the small signs you need to pay more attention to and to help you stay connected to your task is a massive value proposition in business.

4. Ask with clarity. Make sure when you are dealing with business partners, associates, staff and suppliers that you are direct about what you want and what you expect. Lead the relationships.

5. Did not listen? Put it in writing. If you have a situation where you have not been heard, then put it in writing. If the person does not "listen" and amend when you have it in writing, this is your massive signpost. Stop! The test result is fail. Time to set a boundary, say to yourself that you k-no-w and walk away.

6. There are 3 personality subtleties to look out for to avoid if noticed in business partners, associates, staff and suppliers:

•   The Yes Paralyser - This person is excellent at agreeing and saying "yes" and yet fails to take any action or follow through. They paralyse progress in your business as their inaction is detrimental to success. It can take years to release a serial yes paralyser from your business because they are personable, friendly, and loyal and often have the illusion of reliability. They also achieve very little and are a drain on resources.

•   The 180 Opposer - This person will have the exact opposite view to you most of the time. They always say no before they say yes to any ideas or instructions and will tell you what cannot be achieved. The way their mind works is they have to be the instigator and the good brains behind an idea or concept. In unusual ways, they are seeking credit; they will tell you how the success in your business is all about their efforts and work strategies. Often they are excellent producers, the risk is they can take your business off purpose if you allow them to steer too frequently and the direction will be the opposite of where you want to go.

- The Smiling Contaminant - This person is lovely to your face, you think you have a trusted person in them and yet what they feel and sometimes say to others about you is nothing but negative.

What if you find you are unable to make the tough decisions to be discerning and move people on by saying k-no-w and sticking to your guns?

This is excellent timing to consider any secondary gain you may be receiving from remaining in arrangements that are apparently not serving you. Consider some mentoring or assistance to help you in your leadership physiology and communication.

K-no-wing when to let go of business arrangements and people, being able to find personality subtleties and become discerning as you stick to your guns is essential for your success.

CHAPTER 14
VANISHING CLIENTS

Do you ever feel upset about "losing" clients? Can't understand why? I seem to hear this all the time. I'm going to show you why this happens, and how to do something positive about it.

In leadership, you are in charge of what you're doing. The best way to keep clients is to make sure you are well ahead of what the requirements are, in order for you to have that level of leadership. There are certain steps you really need to be taking to make sure people stay with you as clients. In the first step you need to always seek to understand them. This is the fundamental of any relationship you have, whether it be business or personal.

As I say in Chapter One of The Lateral-Thinking Entrepreneur - 33 Principles for Expansive Leadership. The second step you need to do with your clients is, of course, to give them what they want and also what they need. You need to check in and make sure you're doing this in your business.

The third step is you need to continually build trust and respect with your clients. This is a very important aspect of keeping them from vanishing.

In the fourth step, you need to be truly engaged. This means you need to be very focused on them when they're in care with you, or when you're meeting with them. This makes them feel important.

In the fifth step, you need to be courageous and always speak your truth with them. Don't filter. Make sure you are honest, but obviously in a caring and professional manner.

The sixth step is to be aligned with your true self. For others to follow your lead, you need to practice this every day in your work.

The seventh step is to lead by example. This is the first step in preventing clients from vanishing.

I want to ask you something. Doormat? Bottomless pit? Or High road? Which of these three do you think best defines you? What I find with most people I work with – consultants who want to improve their business – is when it comes to vanishing clients, they think about it in one of three ways.

The first way is they consider themselves as the consultant or the practitioner, to be a doormat. In this I feel you're being very weak.

It isn't leadership to be a doormat and allow your clients to decide what they want, rather than you taking the lead and showing them what they need and being in control of the relationship you have with them. Are you a doormat?

The next person I come across is what I call the bottomless pit. This is the consultant or practitioner who is quite arrogant and makes it all about themselves. In other words, they're really not being of service to their clients.

They feel their clients should make the effort to come to them without actually stepping out and making the door wide open, to enable that client to feel they're an important part of the relationship.

This comes down to communication and making sure you are able to build trust and respect. If you feel like you have an arrogant attitude toward clients who don't come back, then you need to be thinking about whether you're behaving like a bottomless pit.

The third category I call the high road. In the high road you have the leader. What happens with the leader is they know, with every client, that they're in until that client says they are out.

The high road leader will chase somebody to the other side of the world in order for them to know they are cared for, and important to that consultant or practitioner. I think it's very important, when it comes to vanishing clients, to decide which of the three you are.

You'll find you do tend to be toward one of them. The best place for you is to take the high road and be the leader, and take a balanced, trusting, and respectful approach to how you retain your clients.

There are a couple of things you need to do in order to create the situation where your clients don't vanish. First of all, of course, you want to keep them on schedule from the very beginning. If that doesn't happen, you always need to contact them.

How you contact them is very important. Your contact with your clients is never to be in touch with them to say, "Hey, you need to come back in." Whenever you pick up the phone or contact a client to find out why they haven't made another appointment with you, you have one purpose.

That purpose is to seek to understand, and to go back through all the checkpoints of you making sure you have created the right relationship to lead people. Have you understood them, given them what they need, built trust and respect?

Are you truly engaged, being courageous, aligned with your true self, and living by example? These are the questions you need to ask yourself when you contact somebody.

When you speak to them to ascertain why they're not using your services at that moment, you want to seek to understand what's going on with their life. It may be that they no longer require your services, and that's fine.

You want to make sure that you keep in touch with people so that they know that you care about them. Sometimes, I think it's great to check in with people. Other times you want to be more direct with them.

In my chiropractic practice, when we call our clients to find out where they're up to if we haven't seen them for a little while, we call it a care call. Our outcome is actually to do nothing more than care for that person.

Sometimes, people are so busy in their lives that they just don't have time to come and see you. It's nothing against you. They just don't have time.

Picking up the phone or sending them a message and letting them know you care about them and they have popped into your mind is a very important way of bringing them back into care when they're ready.

What I also find happens, especially in the healthcare industry, is that people who haven't been educated in terms of what they really need for their health tend to drop out of care when they just simply feel better.

Other people feel embarrassed to contact you after they've dropped out of care because they feel as though they will be reprimanded for the fact they haven't stayed in care. Perhaps their injury or their condition has been exacerbated by their inability to stay on track.

It's really important you always embrace people no matter where they're at. However they show up, you never make them feel bad about the fact they may have missed a few appointments or not seen you for a year.

Always have your door open and the most important thing you can do to maintain that is to ensure you keep following up with people and let them know you care, regardless of whether they come to see you or not.

Here are some things you can do in order to plan and make sure you follow up with people who haven't been in for a while. My first suggestion is you write scripts, scripts about what you're going to say when you pick up the phone, SMS, or write to people.

Make sure those scripts are designed to seek to understand, and are designed just to touch base with people and let them know you care. Next you need to choose how, when, and after what time frame you're going to contact people.

For this I suggest creating a system, a system that enables you to know what you're doing every week, month, quarter, and year in terms of following up people.

You need a database that lets you extract the information on clients who you haven't seen over a certain period of time. This way you know who to contact and when to contact them. Creating a system of how to contact people who haven't been in for a while is a terrific way of keeping in touch and re-engaging with them.

Thirdly, you need to realise this is human-to-human communication in action. Put your best foot forward, and be the leader. You're caring for another human being here.

You're not being a bully asking them to come back in against their will. What you are doing is contacting them to let them know you care. It's very important you take that foot forward when you do this exercise.

In the worst case scenario, you may contact somebody and say to them, "Hey, I haven't seen you for a while, and I want to check in and see how you are," and they don't come in.

What they might do is say to the next person, "You'll never believe who was on the phone. That was my consultant, my doctor, my health-care practitioner, contacting me to let me know they care and to find out how I am."

It's so lovely to know people care. That's all you are doing when you're dealing with a vanishing client.

If you adopt this from the position of being a leader and seek to understand, you will find you create a beautiful energy between yourself and your clients. This will always be valuable for your business.

CHAPTER 15
EDUCATING CLIENTS

D o you ever get a sense sometimes when you're dealing clients they're just not interested in the step-by-step you want to show them? This happens really often, and what I find with this is these clients are often "what" learners, meaning they need to know facts. What they want to hear from you is that you really know your stuff.

In this chapter, I show you how to educate your clients effectively and make sure they become amazing ambassadors for your business. It's important to do this in your business, because it gives you specialist status. It makes your clients know you are educated and at the top of your field. It also keeps them engaged.

People prefer to refer to professionals who they feel are very knowledgeable. So, sharing your knowledge is an important part of making sure you get referrals. Being really good at using facts and figures to share information and educate your clients also spreads good information throughout your community. Most importantly, I feel educating people is a gift and a wonderful thing you can do, as a professional, every day in your working life.

Statistics show that about 22 percent of learning happens through information and observation. What this means is that education is extremely important because you're going to find that at least 22 percent of the people you deal with in your business will want to know the facts in order to feel comfortable with engaging your services for a long period of time.

The best way to educate people is to get a yes response from them before you even start sharing some facts and figures with them. This way, you know your client is truly engaged in what you're educating them on. A great way to do this is to refer to something that is important to that client, and then give them an educational fact.

It might be they are in your medical practice and have a certain condition. You can turn around to say to them, "Did you know that 50 percent of people have this condition?" These are the sorts of facts that really help people to understand you know what you're talking about and you can do a terrific job.

When you're working out how to educate your clients, the best thing to do is to look at the list of problems or opportunities your clients present on a daily basis to you in business. These are the subjects you want to educate yourself on. Learn all the industry statistics in relation to what is presented most in your business by your clients.

In order to educate yourself, you can go on the Internet, but I also suggest going to courses, because I think courses are a very important part of keeping your energy up and you have the cutting edge information you need.

I like the idea of sending what I call "guess what?" letters to your clients. In a guess-what letter, you are sharing information you've learned in a course or through your studies. It's a really terrific way of spreading information to people and adding a high level of value in what you do.

Every month, I suggest you create your own information and fact list to use with your clients in your practice or in your business. This way you keep your topics relevant to the people you're dealing with, but you can continue to educate on a particular theme every month.

This is an important part of you making sure people view you as a specialist and know you are continuing to educate yourself. I suggest you find ways to share factual information with your clients every time you meet with them.

This is a terrific way of making sure you engage with all learning styles that come into your business. Education is a vital part of you being the professional people most want to see. There is no point taking courses and learning things without finding relevant ways to share it with your clients.

The best thing you can do is for your business is to know the majority of problems and opportunities your clients face, and have factual information you can share with them every time you meet.

CHAPTER 16
SETTING AND INCREASING YOUR FEES

Your fees and increasing your fees is a very important part of what you do in your business. So often I find there's a lot of concern around what to charge clients and when to increase fees. It's really important you listen to information on this in order to make sure you establish your business properly and you charge the right fee for your services.

In this chapter, I show you how to set your fees and when to increase them. I want to share a story with you about one of my clients. He came to me because he wanted to grow his business and he was finding he was going backwards, and he wasn't progressing. He'd been consulting in his industry for more than 10 years.

We sat down and had a big discussion about what he was doing and how he was doing it. I asked him, "When was the last time you increased your fees?" I discovered it was 10 years. He had not increased his fees once. Yet we discussed that in 10 years the price of petrol had gone up. The price of a cup of coffee had gone up. The price of a stamp to send a letter had almost doubled. And my client had not increased his fees once in 10 years.

He was actually going backwards. Backwards because he wasn't even increasing his fees in line with the consumer price index and the increase in costs he had to pay for basic services as a consumer. He was not convinced this was an important thing, so we sat down and did some very basic mathematics on it.

We worked out had he just increased his fees by a small percentage, just six percent a year over the 10 year period; he would have increased his earnings by over $450,000 over that period of time. That's a tremendous difference in his quality of living based on the fact he was going backwards in his fee charges. Thankfully, I had some resources that could help him work out how to set his fees properly and how to increase them.

In my business, I increase our fees every year. On the first of February every year we have a price increase. That price increase enables us to continue to provide our services at reasonable fees, and it also enables us to be able to progress as a business and make sure we stay ahead of where all of our expenses are coming from as our outgoings increase over time. We've been in business now for more than 20 years. This is an important business principle we consider to be normal in how we go about our daily business.

When you increase your prices every year, the advantage is you only have to do it in very small increments. This is, of course, really palatable to your clients. If you don't increase your prices frequently, it's almost like you're being passive aggressive when you get to the point when you have to increase your prices and you're so behind you have to increase them significantly. And this really does cause problems for some of your clients.

In my chiropractic business, we have the one dollar per service rule. On the first of February every year we increase every service we give by one dollar. It's as simple as that. In other businesses of course the margin needs to be different and that's because it will depend on what you charge for your services and also what your increased costs are of business on a year-on-year basis.

Some industries have increased costs at different times because services change. In other businesses, you may be required to buy new technology and you may need to plan for this. If you are definitely adding technology to what you do, then of course, you need to factor this into what you charge your clients and make sure your clients are paying or you are offsetting your cost against this for the additional services you are now provide them.

How do you set your prices? The first thing you need to do is research your industry. Have a really good look at what other people are charging in your industry to make sure your figures and your prices work within what the industry is offering.

Then consider how you specialise and how you differentiate from your competition. Be sure you look at this very carefully so you set your price properly for where you feel you sit in the market.

If you're new to business, you may want to start a little bit lower. If you do this, there's a very important criteria I'm going to show you now. You need to create thresholds when you set your price slightly lower than what you feel your services are actually worth. As soon as you reach those thresholds, you need to immediately put your price up for the next client. Sometimes when a business is establishing, I'll suggest setting a price.

Then when that business gets to a certain number of clients per week or per month, I say to that business, "You now need to increase your prices for the next clients who come through." You can often get away with this by calling it an introductory offer for your first clients and then keep the clients at this price while you increase your price for new clients who come in after you've reached your thresholds.

It's really important to increase your prices to what you feel the market should be if you start off a little bit lower. It's OK to start off lower as long as you do increase your prices after you've reached your thresholds.

The purpose of increasing your prices on a regular basis is to ensure your business stays profitable and you can always cover your expenses. You need to appreciate that the costs of what you pay for services to run your business and run your life will always go up.

If you are not increasing your prices on a yearly basis, you will go backwards. Price increases are so essential, yet I find many businesses fail to do this, which is troubling.

Back to my client who hadn't increased his fees in 10 years. We worked out a strategy where he could go back to his clients and offer them packages at a great price, but that were an increased price on what he had been charging over the 10 year period. He was able to do this by letting his clients know that within a three month period the price would be going up quite significantly.

He wanted to give them an advantage to get into continuing to use his services before his prices went up. A number of clients purchased this and for the rest of his clients he simply took the prices up and put in a strategy where he was increasing his prices year-on-year thereafter.

He felt so much better about his business. Even though his hours hadn't changed and the number of clients he saw each week didn't change, how he felt about his business shifted enormously when he realised the revenue he had missed out on by forgetting and neglecting to increase his prices year-on-year.

Increasing your prices annually is crucial to your business. It's very challenging when you don't increase your prices over a number of years and the consumer price index changes which mean your costs go up. Then you get into a situation where you're totally behind and you need to increase your prices faster than the market can handle.

If you haven't increased your prices for a long time, now is the time to go and have a look at it and put in place a strategy that sees you increase your prices by at least five to six percent every year going forward.

CHAPTER 17
CREATING PACKAGES FOR YOUR SERVICES

I'm often told how unpredictable and scary it can be being a consultant in your own business. A lot of my clients want to know how they can predict their income sources, and make sure they have a really good understanding of how their business is going to track for the year ahead.

I'm regularly asked how people can do this with ease and I have some real clarity on how this can be planned. I show you how your can do this in this chapter by creating packages for your services.

Packaging your product and your services is nothing more than presenting a proposal of bundled services in an attractive or advantageous way for your clients. You want to keep this simple, and make sure your client sees there is value in them purchasing an up-front package.

This can come in a number of ways. It can come in services that can be used on an individual basis, over a period of time. Or for example, it can come in the form of a retainer, where you give your client an advantage for booking your services for an entire year.

Why would you want to do this in your business? There are a number of reasons why this is advantageous. It increases your certainty of income by making sure you understand who your long-term clients are. They are committed and will continue to use your services on a long-term basis.

Clients on packages have an increased level of commitment and loyalty to you. They tend to use your services ahead of somebody else's because they know they have a package that is prepaid with you. You will have a better ability to plan your time, knowing who your package clients are and the time you need to allocate for them.

Better still, when you plan your time carefully, you can actually assist your clients who are on packages by allocating their appointments over a period of time, so you know exactly when they're coming in to utilise their entire package.

Providing packages is very good for cash flow predictability in your business. Another advantage is it takes the transaction out of the relationship. In other words, when your client is coming for your services, the transaction doesn't seem to be about the payment this time around. It is simply about them coming in, utilising your services or connecting with you, and then leaving again with the transaction part already done. This has a lot of advantages in your relationships with your clients.

Another great reason for creating packages is that it rewards loyalty, and it enables people to have even better value for your services. When deciding how to put together your packages, look at the big companies for the lead.

I look at organisations like telecommunication companies with mobile phone and data packages; products like Foxtel, how gyms run their memberships; and I like to model their systems.

I go to the organizations I think do a really good job of packages in a particular area, and look at their terms and conditions. I think about what I like that they are providing, and I use this as a way to create a bundle or to put together a package that is going to be advantageous for the client I'm working with.

It's important you get a good understanding of what you like when you buy a package. You don't want any hidden surprises, and if this is important to you, then you want to make sure work with integrity. Give your clients what you would expect in terms of how you would like to be treated if you were purchasing a package as well.

There are so many organisations out there that offer packages for their clients. Researching this can be a very good way of determining how you could put together a terrific package for your business.

How do you put together the package after you've done the research? The first thing you want to do is think about two packages only, to get started. I strongly recommend you review the chapter on Choices versus Dilemma to find out more about the importance of taking a simple approach to your offer. You don't want to give your clients too many options when you're putting together a package. You either want to offer them Package One or Package Two, and that's it. Having too much choice creates a dilemma. When there's a dilemma people tend not to make a decision.

Look at how you can bundle your package for value. In other words, is there a discount offered as part of a package? How much is that discount? I suggest 10 to 15 percent is a really good advantage. Or you can add additional services in for free as part of the package?

These are ways in which you can bundle your services together. The most important thing is that you offer value for money in what you do. The next thing is to create very easy and clear marketing about your packages.

If you have a number of terms and conditions, refer to these and put the details on a page on your website for terms and conditions which are easy to find. In your marketing material, you can simply refer your clients to your website for them to have a detailed look at what the terms and conditions are of each package.

Keep the marketing very simple and clear, this enables people to make a quick decision. It should take them no more than 30 seconds to 1 minute to be able to determine what the packages are and how they will work for them. Write them so a twelve year old could make a decision. This will make it much easier for people to make a decision on whether they would like to purchase a package or not.

You need to offer your packages at peak-satisfaction moments with your clients. The best time to offer a package is when a client is telling you how much they enjoy your services, and how much benefit they are receiving from working with you. This provides the perfect opportunity to say to them, "Do you know what? I have a package that you may be interested in purchasing so you can use my services on an on-going basis at a discounted rate." Or, "I really enjoy working with you as well. I would like to go on a retainer so we can continue to work together on a monthly basis. I can offer you a discount if you would like to do that." It's important to always choose the moments at which your client has come to you and said how much they like and appreciate you. Use that as your in-road to offer a package to them. In this state, they're more likely to want to purchase your package. If you're continually offering packages to people at moments where they're not in a satisfaction frame of mind then you're going to find it difficult and you're going to feel like you're selling. When you offer it at a time when your client is telling you how much they like working with you and how much they enjoy using your services, then you will find it is a much easier transaction.

You need to be very careful about how you manage the administration of your packages. Ensuring that you keep this simple, but also keep it very accurate, is a very important part of being professional in how you put these together. Before you even consider offering packages to your clients, make sure that you have the administration of these packages well sorted in your business, so you know exactly how you're going to manage them. At any moment, your client will want to know where they're up to with their package. It's important for you to have accurate data. I see many small businesses getting this completely wrong. It's a real worry when the client has no idea how many package items they have used and when the consultant themselves has no idea either this is a recipe for disaster. Make sure you get your administration right and your systems in place before you even offer your packages to your clients.

What if a client wants a refund as part of their package? In my business, I find the refund rate is very low. I have a very direct and genuine policy when it comes to refunds and it is this: If, at any time, a client in our business who has purchased a package wants a refund for any reason, we offer the refund without any hesitation. In fact, our policy is to give them the refund directly into their bank account within 24 hours of their request. My policy here is very important for the way in which our clients view our business and of what they say about us even after they are no longer a client of ours. I want any client, regardless of whether they have been on a package or not, to always have an amazing experience with us. I feel I have no right to hold onto anyone's money if they've purchased a package and decide halfway through it they don't want that package anymore. I think there is a terrific marketing story in giving people a lot of ease around making sure you refund them with ease, and in a very ethical way, as soon as they ask for it. In fact, in our business we have a less than two percent request for refunds on packages. This is a tiny percentage of our business.

I feel our refund policy is a really positive one, because we put the money directly into the client's bank account. We contact them by letter and thank them for being such an amazing client. We let them know they are always welcome to come back to us at any stage.

In many businesses, the reason why somebody might want a refund halfway through a package is because their life circumstances have changed. For us, it's somebody moving interstate or somebody deciding they have a problem we can no longer help them with. They've needed to go to another professional who can help them even more.

In my business, client satisfaction is number one for me. Whether a client stays with our business or goes somewhere else, I feel they need to be satisfied with our service either way.

We can't help everyone. We will always do our best to help everyone, and in some circumstances it may be they need to go to another professional. I want them to go to that professional with the best opinion of us at all times. This means if they have purchased a package from us, I will always give them a refund. I think having this policy in place has been very advantageous for us as a business. Just the energy around it means very few people ask for a refund because they know we will always look after them in the event they want one. This creates no room for animosity, and it also enables our clients to know they can trust us when they purchase a package.

I believe that easy terms and value packages are essential in business and as a consequence many clients purchase packages from our business. I suggest you do the same in your business. See the results of creating client loyalty around having packages that reward your clients, while keeping them in your services over a much longer period of time.

CHAPTER 18
DIVERSIFIED INCOME SOURCES

When you trade your time for income, it may seem as though there is little leverage for you to increase your earnings. This doesn't need to be so.

There are some clever ways in which you can diversify your income sources. Some of these won't take any of your time. Others will not cost you anything.

Some of them just involve you being very clever about making sure you're giving your clients a variety of services they can utilise from you instead of coming to you for one service and then going elsewhere for something else you could be offering.

It's time to be business smart about this. What I know from working with my clients is that you could increase your income by up to 15 to 20 percent by diversifying your income sources.

One day, I was working with a healthcare practitioner who was concerned about his time. He wanted to increase his income. We were looking at ways in which he could increase his income while at the same time providing easy, relevant, and value-added services for his clients.

He was very worried it was going to take a lot of effort. Surprisingly, what he found was that he missed out on opportunities his clients were already going elsewhere for.

The best way to sit down and work out what the diversified income sources are that you could put into your business is to think about your clients and consider what they may be going elsewhere for you could be offer in your business.

For example, I have often worked with people who are in the beauty and hair care industry who by adding in a complementary service provider into their business, are able to keep their clients in the business for longer and, at the same time, provide services they would otherwise have to go elsewhere for.

I also find in this industry that having a range of quality products to sell clients is a terrific idea. There's a proviso, though. Many of these products simply sit on the shelf with a practitioner or service provider failing to actually offer them actively to their clients every time they're in.

The trick here is to always make sure you actually offer the product to your client and show it to them rather than allowing it to just sit on the shelf. Allow them to make a personal choice about whether they would like it or not.

As a consultant, you help your clients in many areas. One of those areas is to make sure that what they take home and use in their home environment to compliment your services is actually going to enhance their experience with you.

To have it sit on the shelf may be counterintuitive and may not provide you with what you actually need in order to give that client the highest level of service.

When you diversify your income, you are actually increasing variety to create increased revenue streams. That's the only thing you need to consider when you think about doing this in your business.

There are five key areas in which I always look when working with clients to determine whether we could find some increased variety of income streams to assist them to grow their business.

Complementary Products

The first area is complementary products. By this I mean products that directly enhance the service being provided. For a healthcare practitioner, that may be a range of quality vitamin supplements or food supplies that clients should have in order to maintain their health.

It could also be other things such as sporting equipment, foam rollers, or items that a practitioner would normally recommend a client go and purchase somewhere else.

Anything you suggest your client goes to another store to buy is something you could be offering in your business for them to purchase from you instead. The key is always to offer it to the client at the right moment and in a relevant context.

If you feel that clients need to be taking dietary supplements, then you need to be looking at this in the context of their health and your practice. Make sure you carefully prescribe to them exactly what they need and what you believe they should have as their healthcare practitioner and the leader in their healthcare solution.

Again, there's no point simply having it sit on the shelf and enabling your client to make their own choices. This is about you taking an active role in offering products to your clients whom you know will complement and enhance their experience of working with you.

New Services

The second area in which you can increase your diversification of income is to provide new services. Sometimes this may be a service you offer yourself as an added service in your service menu, or you may bring somebody else into your business to do this.

I was working with a hairdresser once who had space in her business, and she decided to bring in a nail artist. This meant that while she was doing somebody's hair, they could also have their nails done at the same time.

Some clients loved this, and the nail artist did very, very well. The deal she had put together with the nail artist meant it was no cost to the hairdresser to have the nail artist there. In fact, all she was doing was paying her a commission of about 15 percent on all the clients she was seeing.

This was a terrific win/win solution that didn't cost the hairdresser any extra time, and it enabled them to make the best use of space and also have an increased income source without actually having to do any additional work.

There are many businesses in which new services can be added. Healthcare practices, for instance, can offer things like massage therapy, reflexology, and other services by having another practitioner come in and use space that isn't being otherwise used for consultations in order to have these services provided.

The exchange needs to be very simple in terms of what the additional practitioner pays you for using your space. Don't complicate this. Make it easy. This is a diversified income source, and you don't want to have responsibilities for keeping that person busy or having to set up their business for them.

All you want to do is offer something else of quality to your clients, while at the same time just creating another 10, 15, or 20 percent of income into your daily takings.

In providing new services to your clients, perhaps you could offer a different service.

For instance, I have a number of chiropractors I work with who offer things like Gaitscan where they're actually assessing people's feet in order to determine whether they need a custom made orthotic. They then sell these orthotics to their clients based on the results the clients get from the foot scan.

These sorts of services don't take a lot of time for the professional, and once you are trained in how to use them, they can be very easy to implement in your practice. The advantage of this is that you provide your clients with a greater chance of them having even better health outcomes from your services.

In my practice, we do offer Gaitscan, and we find it takes the practitioner 15 to 20 minutes in order to do it. Whether the client decides they need the orthotic or not, or the practitioner decides to recommend it, isn't the point.

The point is this is a diversified income source that, more importantly than anything, enhances the healing experience for the client. A client needing an orthotic would otherwise have to go to a different professional in order to have this.

Why not offer a service that is complementary to what you do and enhances the outcomes for your client at the same time? I work with a personal trainer who has decided to offer babysitting services for her mothers who come for personal training services.

What she does is she has a babysitter who assists the mothers. She takes a small commission on the hours that the babysitter works. This way she gets to keep her clients in personal training while they have somebody who can look after their baby while they're having their session with the personal trainer?

The mothers find this amazing. Paying an extra $20 to $25 an hour for this service is fantastic because it still enables them to have a training session whereas otherwise, they may need to engage a babysitter for three to four hours in order for them to go out and do a one-hour gym session.

These are great ways in which you can diversify your income by really determining what your client needs and offering it within your own environment rather than expecting them to go elsewhere for it. It sets you apart as a leader and a professional in your field when you are able to do this.

Affiliate Programs

Another area in which you can diversify your income is to offer affiliate programs. I know a lot of people get very nervous about working as an affiliate for another organisation, but there are some great advantages of doing this.

Firstly, I find there are a lot of affiliate programs that offer products of extremely high quality. The business structure of an affiliate program actually means you can purchase these items at a very good price.

Recommending products to your clients through affiliate programs also has a terrific advantage for your cash flow in your business. When you work as an affiliate for another organisation recommending their products, you simply receive a commission check from them on a weekly or monthly basis.

There's no financial outlay for you, and this is a fantastic thing for cash flow in your business. When you're an affiliate for another organisation, that organisation supplies the product directly to your client so you're not required to hold stock.

This can be a terrific way of grow your business. I have seen a number of businesses grow by even 20 to 30 percent when they find the right affiliate programs that work well for diversifying the income for their business.

There are lots of different ways in which you can do this, and it's very good to research what affiliate programs are available that offer complementary products and services for what you do. This is an excellent way of doing business, and I highly recommend it for diversifying income.

Group Events

Another way in which you can diversify your income is to look at ways in which you could bring small groups of people together within your business from your client base.

I know some businesses offer special nights like movie nights where they're showing a documentary that's relevant to their industry or where they bring in a guest speaker. These evenings can be a fantastic way to diversify your income.

Having a guest speaker come in and charging a small fee for an evening event can be quite a great way of growing. It also means that clients are likely to bring other people to your business, who otherwise would not be customers.

These people might create a relationship with you and become clients of yours in the process. If you are looking to run seminars, movie nights, documentary nights, or bring in guest speakers, remember it's always important to charge a fee for these services. Don't do it for free.

It's very likely that people will simply not turn up or value it unless they're paying for it. You don't need to charge a lot of money, but making a few hundred or a $1,000 for an event can be an excellent way to diversify and increase your income.

If you do these 6 to 12 times a year, you can see how your income could increase quite dramatically. Your ability to connect with new members of your community in order to create a larger client base also increases.

These are some ideas I talked to my practitioner about, and we came up with a number of areas in which he could diversify his income. He had space he could offer to another practitioner, and he started by doing this and filled that space at times when he wasn't using it.

He also offered products and services and increased his range here. He had a few snack products on the counter. More importantly, he actually deliberately recommended and prescribed supplements to his clients.

The uptake was much higher than he thought. Not everyone bought the products, but that's fine. He was at least offering them in a way that was ethical, credible, and quality, meaning he felt more confident that his clients would be doing the right things at home to look after their health when he wasn't with them.

He also decided to conduct some seminar nights. For this, he hired a small cinema and brought in a few guest speakers and showed some interesting documentaries he felt would be relevant to his market.

This was highly beneficial for his business, and it helped him to grow. He has an extra 20 percent of income every year based on the ways in which he has diversified his income sources.

This was easier to do than he had first thought, and the benefit for him in terms of marketing has been incredible as well.

When you diversify your income, the only thing you really need to consider is who are my clients and what are they purchasing elsewhere or what services are they using elsewhere that they could instead be using inside my business?

How could I offer these services to my clients and enable them to get these services from me instead of going somewhere else? How could I make life more convenient for my clients?

When you answer these questions, you will find some terrific ways to diversify your income sources.

CHAPTER 19
NON-ESSENTIAL
CONVERSATION

As you read this book, you are getting a sense of how to reverse engineer your success. In other words, how to look at things laterally and work out a way of doing something that is perhaps, very obvious, but not being done by a lot of people.

This is one of my success secrets in business. The ability to look at how everybody else is doing something mundane and reverse the thinking to find a simplified and easier way to do it.

In this chapter, I share with you the advantages of non-essential conversation. What I see with non-essential conversation are opportunities for true connection that is completely missed by so many people today.

What is non-essential conversation? It's incidental, unnecessary, informal exchange of thoughts and information.

I consider non-essential conversation is something that is completely missing for many people today, and yet as a leader, you can have an amazing impact on people by understanding the importance of non-essential conversation, and actually use it to your advantage in business.

More than that, you create a feeling of rapport with people who you never thought was possible. With this comes a high level of trust and respect that enables you to take them on an amazing journey.

Why is non-essential conversation so important? Today, we've become very obsessed with social media, distraction and looking at our smartphones all the time. We think we are connected and the truth is we are living in our heads and on a screen. It's interesting sometimes to just sit near a street corner in the city and watch the number of people who are connected to their mobile phones and looking down the whole time. Even at my daughter's gymnastics competition recently I witnessed parents missing the moment of watching their child "live" because they were busy taking a video of the performance on a smartphone.

I was reading an interesting article earlier this year about the number of traffic accidents involving pedestrians who were using mobile phones. It's really quite alarming how disconnected we have become from the world around us when we are connected to our screens.

We may think that using all this technology is actually helping us to be connected, and I think differently. I feel that it is actually helping people to be disconnected.

As a consequence of this, I think there are some terrific advantages in finding incidental and unnecessary times to have an exchange of thoughts and information with people that enables them to be able to connect with another human being.

As a consultant or business owner, utilising this in your business is also a terrific advantage for you in increasing the level of human connection you have with your clients. This is something that will be refreshing for them, and will assist them on many levels.

Having non-essential conversation is a part, for me, of VIP service. It's actually showing people you care beyond just pushing them through a system, or a consultation, or appointment that is time-based and based on them just merely receiving the outcome of your services.

When you take it to the next level by being willing to have a conversation with them that is perhaps, outside the scope of their appointment, you are showing that you care for another human being.

This will also help to increase the happiness of other people. It's amazing how people today find it so exciting and so liberating to have a conversation with somebody. This is an important part of true leadership.

In my practice, as you will know, I am not a practitioner. Yet I go in there and sit in the reception area at times to have non-essential conversation with the clients who are coming through to see the doctors. I find this is an uplifting experience, and I absolutely love it, as do the clients.

It's become such an important part of our business that I've taught our receptionists and assistants the art of non-essential conversation, and enabled them to have the opportunity to walk out from behind the desk, to sit down next to a client and have a chat with them.

With this, we're having a chat about anything and everything, whatever might be happening in the world, the weather, how that patient's feeling, anything. It's a non-essential conversation that is designed to show we care.

We take the time to listen to people, and to connect with them. It's extraordinary the feedback we get from this. I'm shocked to hear how many people in their own homes don't have conversations with the people they live with.

There's such an emphasis on disconnect through technology, computers and television that people are not even sitting down to have a conversation anymore. We've taken this as a true opportunity for human connection in our business, and the results of this are astounding.

When you are willing to have non-essential conversation with people, you are showing true leadership. This is an important part of you developing your business.

What are the qualities of non-essential conversation that make you a leader? Here are the qualities I look for in leaders, and I see in the people I work with who are leaders in their profession.

The first is honesty. What's real is real, and when you sit down and have a non-essential conversation with somebody, you have to understand their model of the world. With this, their opinion may not be the same as yours. Yet respecting their opinion is a really important part of you showing leadership.

As a leader, the best leaders I work with know how to delegate. When you're having a non-essential conversation with somebody, it may be that something comes up they want to share with you that's important to your business, and you can then find an opportunity to be able to provide the level of service they're looking for.

Sometimes this means you will be able to find somebody else you could delegate to in order to enable you to provide a higher level of service to your client. Often this will come through non-essential conversation.

Communication is a very important leadership quality, and your ability to talk to anyone and everyone should be a priority in what you do every day of your life. Leaders also show commitment, and with this they show commitment to the people they lead.

By you the ability to have non-essential conversation with your clients, you are show them that you have a commitment beyond your scope of work that enables you to really take them on the journey of where they need to go.

Leaders also have a positive attitude. I find one of the most important things about non-essential conversation is the ability to make somebody's day.

Often I will have to take a very positive high road with someone I'm speaking to, if they're coming across with a story that has saddened them, upset them, or if they're dealing with some personal issues in their life.

The opportunity to help somebody at this level is really energising, and it is an incredible gift to give to another human being. Leaders also show a high level of creativity, and when you're having a non-essential conversation with somebody, believe me, there are times when you need to be extremely creative and flexible.

It's a wonderful thing to have this quality, and to be available to people at this level. All good leaders have intuition.

Sometimes having a non-essential conversation with somebody will be because the demeanour they're showing you at that moment in time lets you know they need something they're not articulating.

So often today, people walk through life with all this baggage they are unable to express to another human being. Having the intuition to sit down and have a conversation with somebody can be a great opportunity for healing somebody at a level you never thought imaginable.

Leaders also inspire. Sitting down with somebody and inspiring them through non-essential conversation is an important part of you being a leader. How do you do this? It's really easy. You take the time to look somebody in the eye and have a conversation with them.

Just be intuitive, whatever comes up. You might ask them a question, or you might ask for their opinion on something, or you might just let them speak. Connecting with them initially through looking at them in the eye is a terrific way to start a conversation.

What you are doing here is ascertaining from them what their model of the world is, and to find an area of their life in which you can show leadership, in which you can inspire them, in which you can have human connection with them that they otherwise may not be having.

This has a profound effect on the nervous system. When people feel heard and understood, they tend to be happier, and they tend to be more willing to be open. This is an advantage for you in your business.

What if you're having a non-essential conversation with somebody and they don't want to talk? That's fine. Take the time to seek to understand. Some people will not want to have a non-essential conversation with you, and that's fine, but this is about leadership.

This is about setting the right steps in place for you to set your business apart from what other people do. Non-essential conversation and being open to it is a big part of your success in business.

CHAPTER 20
SMS AND PHONE CALL MAGIC

F ollow up and keeping in contact with clients is a great way to increase your rapport. The challenge is that it sometimes takes time and a lot of planning. Many business people find this isn't easy to do. I'm going to show you an extremely easy and very powerful way in which you can follow up your clients every day.

I call this my SMS and phone call magic. I'm going to show you the simplest marketing you will ever do. When you are a leader, contacting your clients after their appointment and consultations with you, by SMS or phone call, is something that is absolutely profound in terms of their opinion of your services. You have no idea the impact you have on another human being when you contact them outside of the time they're expecting to hear from you.

Today, even though we may feel connected, so many people are disconnected. Knowing that whoever they work with, as a consultant or practitioner, cares about them – beyond their appointment – is something that has a profound impact on someone's ability to get on with their life and feel the true advantage of working with you.

When you actually sit down and work out how much time this takes, you'll realise it's not about time. It's about planning. I'm going to show you a very easy way to plan this into your day, so the last 15 to 20 minutes of your day is the most powerful marketing you will ever do.

My suggestion is that you have a memo in your notes on your phone, or otherwise a book or diary, that you can jot some notes down during the day as you think about your clients, or as something comes up in their consultation with you. You're just making a small note, so you don't have to think about what you're going to do at the end of the day.

Write it down. Then, at the end of the day, make a decision who to call and who to SMS. Sometimes, people prefer to do this the following morning rather than the day of the consultation with their client or the day of them thinking about their client – whatever works best for you.

Find 15 to 20 minutes a day, where you're going to sit down and do your SMS and phone call magic. It's very simple. All you need to do is think of something that was important that came up in the consultation with them, or just let them know you are thinking about them and wish them success in what you've worked with them on.

My partner is a fitness instructor, and he's been in the industry for more than 25 years. Every morning, after he has started his day, he SMS's the clients from the day before. He SMSs one line to them, and it is this, "How are you feeling post-workout?" Every client who's had a session with him will get that SMS, and they will respond to him and let him know what's happening.

Some people won't respond. Some people will pick up the phone and ring him, some of his clients send the funniest responses of all time and some people will ignore the SMS! The point is that he's thinking about client the following day and follows up and checks in with them to make sure they've had a good session, and their results are going well and are on track. This has a profound impact on his business and long term retention of clients.

In my chiropractic practice, after a client has been treated for the first time, the practitioner will phone that client, often on their way home from work, and check in with them to see how they're going after their first appointment. This is an important part of showing how much we care. In addition, they will randomly choose clients throughout the day they want to message because something has come up.

It may be something came up in non-essential conversation with that client during their session, and they want to wish them luck for something, or let them know they were thinking about them in the context of something that's going on in their life. It actually doesn't matter. This is about human connection and taking the leadership to contact somebody out of context.

When you decide who to contact, you need to have a system. The first thing you're going to do is have certain things in place that will be part of your system. In other words, in an earlier chapter, we talked about doing regular reviews with clients.

Sometimes that phone call or SMS will be related to the regular review and the decisions that have been made as a consequence of that. At other times, it'll just be to let the client know you care about them and you're thinking about them, in terms of the outcomes they're trying to achieve in their life.

Sometimes the system will be based on something that has come up within a consultation that's a red flag. Maybe the person has an injury or something they're dealing with in their life that you want to make sure they stay on track with. You'll red-flag that and have it as a context in which you are contacting them.

What you are doing is the simplest and most profound form of marketing for your business. You are treating your clients as individuals and by contacting them on a one-on-one basis to let them know that, outside the context of your appointment time with them, you care.

I have a hairdresser who sends messages to her clients at the end of the day to say, "Thank you. It was so beautiful to see you today, and I'm so happy I can be a part of your journey." This is something she does to keep in touch with her clients, and it is beautiful and profound.

What's even more amazing about this is the number of people who will then go and tell another person they received a personal message or phone call from their practitioner and consultant, and how much that has impacted them.

This is a really important part of you showing leadership in your business, and it is by far the simplest marketing you will ever do.

CHAPTER 21
POWERFUL POSTCARDS

Many small business people I work with find marketing isn't easy. The problem is the cost of it can be quite high, and they don't know where to start.

In this chapter, I show you the easiest marketing you will ever do with postcards. I love postcard marketing. I think it is so easy and effective. The thing that is also fantastic about postcard marketing is how few people actually use postcards in the right way.

For me, a postcard is very personal. It's not a flyer. It's not a brochure. It's not an advertisement. A postcard was traditionally used when you were traveling on a holiday or vacation, and you wanted to send somebody a message to let them know what you were up to. Whenever I travel, I make a point of sending postcards to people by snail mail. I send traditional postcards because I love the fact you can receive something from the other side of the world that has a picture, a hand-scribbled message, a stamp, and postmark and has come all that way.

Postcards today are so infrequently used, and yet in business, I think they are a terrific marketing tool – when done properly and in a personal way. There are some really terrific apps you can use in order to make your postcard marketing very easy.

There are a number of websites you can go to, to design your own postcards, and you can have these printed and delivered to your office within a couple of days. The Australian website moo.com.au is a terrific postcard website that enables you to create small batches of postcards, and then have them sent to your office so you can then write them and send them out to your clients.

In addition, the international website, canva.com also provides a terrific postcard creation app, where you can design your own postcard, load your own images and your logo, and have these delivered to your office, so that you can send them to your clients.

I use postcards in my business every day. At the end of the day, I will choose a couple of people who I want to send a postcard to. I just write a short message on that and I pop it in the mail to them, so that they'll receive it in the next few days.

It may be something simple as, "Great session today. It's so terrific to be working with you." It doesn't have to be anything profound. It's the thought that counts. It's taking the time to actually write somebody a postcard and send it.

Some of the most profound marketing I've done is to use postcards at the time when my practitioners in my healthcare business are traveling. When my practitioners are going away on holiday or going to interesting conferences, we create a postcard that enables the practitioner to send the postcards from the other side of the world to their clients, letting them know what they're up to while they're away.

With that type of marketing, there are very clever ways in which you can choose a handwriting font and print a message on the back of the postcard. Even though it's not 100 percent personalised, it still feels as though that person is receiving a personal postcard.

When you use personal postcard marketing, it's not about driving clients back into your practice or back into your business. It's actually just one-on-one communication that is showing the client you care about them. I don't use postcards for offers or for selling things to our clients. I use it for the exact opposite. I use it as an added level of service.

What I think people do when they receive these postcards is they tell other people they have received them. The number of times I have people contact me just to say, "Thank you so much for your postcard," is incredible. What other forms of marketing have this level of response?

People are so bombarded by marketing and sales pitches that when they receive brochures or letters in the mail, they tend to just skim over the top of them and throw them away. But, when you receive a personalised postcard – particularly one that's been handwritten – you tend to look at it in a completely different way.

Another way in which you can create personalised postcards is to use the app from Australia Post in Australia that enables you to upload photographs, and then write personalised messages on your postcard. For less than $3, Australia Post will deliver that postcard anywhere in Australia through their postal service. This is a terrific way of keeping in touch with people. I mentor a number of practitioners and business people who now use this APP every day. At the end of the day, they open their Australia Post postcard app, and decide who they want to send a postcard to. They simply fill in the details on that postcard, and through the online app, post it to their client. Within a couple of days, it's received in the mail like a normal letter. This is a terrific way to get your postcard marketing up and running. In order to work out who to send postcards to, create a list as you go through your day of the people you'd like to contact and why. It could be a simple message about their care or about what you're doing with them, or it could just be to say hello. It actually doesn't matter. What matters is you're taking a personalised approach, and you are doing something toward your marketing every day. You will be amazed at how good this is for your business.

Postcards are powerful when used as I have suggested. You will be very surprised by the number of people who will tell another person they have received a personalised postcard from you.

CHAPTER 22
DRAMA

As a consultant working one-on-one with people, dealing with drama can come with challenges. Clients who have dramatic situations happening in their life can be draining. They always seem to be facing problems.

Some would think your role is to rescue people. I think completely differently. Your role is not to rescue people. It's to empower people. When you try to rescue them, you end up feeling more drained.

Often when I mentor clients, I hear about how drained they feel by the problems faced by their clients. This is because we tend to take on other people's problems as though they are our own.

In this chapter, I show you some interesting information about drama and how you can completely transform your business when you understand drama and how it presents itself with your clients.

I first learned these concepts when studying neuro-linguistic programming and became a trainer of NLP. I thought it was very interesting, as over the years I had seen how drama influenced success in leadership.

In the urban dictionary, drama is described as situations that have relatively easy solutions, but instead of finding that easy solution, the person chooses a negative way to deal with it, and make the problem even worse. This person then looks for someone to rescue them. And to rescue somebody is to take on the act of saving them.

It also involves the role of a persecutor, someone who subjects another person to hostility. In my mind, it also involves the role of a blamer, someone who wants to assign fault to another person when attempting to deal with their own problems.

So often today, we see blaming, critical, oppressive and angry behaviour. This is the persecutor, "It's your fault!" Then we have the rescuer saying, "Let me help you," but what the rescuer actually does is take on the person's problem without making them accountable for it themselves. And, of course, you have the victim who says, "Poor me. Please help me with my problem."

As the leader, the reason you want to understand the dynamics of drama is because it comes at a high emotional cost if you get involved in other people's every day drama. This is no way to lead. All good leaders deal with problem-solving, and it is not about taking on somebody's problems as though they are your own. Nor is it about forcing somebody's will, if they decide they want to stay in drama and continue to be the victim, it is their choice.

Your role in how this works is very important, because while you stay within the victim-rescuer-persecutor role with them, you cannot resolve the situation with your client.

The drama triangle on which this theory is based was developed by Stephen Karpman in 1968 for Alcoholics Anonymous. He mapped conflict situations and realised there were a number of roles people played. He discovered that when people were not taking personal responsibility in conflicts, destructive roles were on display.

Karpman defined these roles as the persecutor, the rescuer, and the victim. In this, he found that most alcoholics had dysfunctional relationships with their family and the people around them. Consequently, every time they stepped into the negative behaviour, it resulted in their selfish needs becoming the focus.

They end up drawing other people into their chaos, usually close family and loved ones, in order to be rescued by them. But in their state of dysfunction, they also end up being the persecutor. What happens over time is people simply swap roles. When the alcoholic is no longer drunk, they become a different role within the situation.

It's very interesting to see how this insight may parallel your experience when you work with your clients. By raising your vibration out of the drama triangle your success in business and leadership can make a phenomenal shift.

Why would you want to do this?

The main reasons you would want to deal with drama in a different way is so you can have more energy; get better results with your clients; and with your assistance enable people to stand in their own power and their own light to resolve their own problems.

The best leaders I work with are people who inspire other people. They don't take on other people's problems as though they are their own. When you trade your time for income and work with clients on a one-on-one basis, it's important you understand the role of the drama cycle and that you can pull yourself out of it.

There are a number of ways in which you can deal with drama with your clients. The first thing to do is become the observer. I look at this as taking a logical level above, in other words, pull yourself out of the situation entirely and look at it like you're watching a movie on a screen. Your purpose in doing this is to understand the different roles people play within this arrangement.

You will see that someone plays the victim, someone plays the rescuer, and someone plays the persecutor. If you have personally become involved in this situation with your client, in other words, if you take on their problem as if it is your own, you will see yourself in that picture, as well. You will notice how you help to foster the dysfunction.

When you step outside of it and watch it like a movie, you see what's at play. You need to appreciate though that some people will always want to stay stuck, and there's nothing you can do to take them out of it. What you can do is stay out of the drama.

I often find it incredibly powerful to go back to the client and ask them this. "OK, I see you are the victim of this situation, and you're finding it difficult to deal with it. I want to take you out of the picture and show you what you are looking at so you can get a real sense of what it feels like to be on the outside looking in. If you listen very carefully to me, you will see what is really going on here. Look at it like a movie on a screen, so you can see all the roles each individual is playing."

Once the person has a real grip on that, you can then take them on a journey to be the creator. The most important fact you want to elicit from them is what they want to create instead. What is it they are looking for? How can you, with your logical levels of understanding above the situation, assist them to get this outcome?

So let's recap here. When your client is sitting in drama, the **only** steps you need to make are to observe like you are watching a movie and empower them to create what they would like instead. You cannot resolve drama from within the drama itself. In other words, if your client gets into dramatic situations and you turn into the rescuer within that environment, you are not serving them.

Many of my clients find this to be a completely counterintuitive way of thinking. Somehow consultants and people working in the service sector, particularly in the healthcare profession, find their role is to help and serve people. They mistakenly think this means to rescue them. Actually, you are a leader, and you guide people out of their problems. You help them find their own solutions which empowers them to take action.

When you take their problems on as though they are your own, you cannot find a solution for them. Even when you deal with somebody's health or the personal choices they make, you cannot actually do the work for them. Consultants don't do the work for other people. Good consultants enable people to do the work themselves.

I believe all roles played in the service industry involve a certain level of drama, and yet you don't need to be drained by this. You can be energised if you simply look at it in a different way, and appreciate your role is to remain outside of the drama.

If you adopt this strategy in your business, you will find powerful insights that get you right to the core of someone's issues, and enable you to facilitate results they never thought possible.

CHAPTER 23
OUTSOURCING

When you trade your time for income, you need to appreciate the importance of the commodity of time. So often, I hear from business people who spend many hours, and sometimes an entire day, doing tasks to manage their business that can be done in a fraction of time through outsourcing. I hear all the time how draining this is, and how difficult this makes it for them to grow and increase their income. These tasks take them away from clients and stop them from being able to progress. It also means they work on tasks not within their area of expertise, and they find this very difficult.

In this chapter, I show you how powerful outsourcing can be when you trade your time for income and need to create more time for yourself to see clients. You see, I believe the best leaders in the world know the secret of including in their business experts in every area they need in order to succeed.

While most business people want to have a handle on everything that is going on in their business, they know the advantage of having people around them who are terrific in their own area and field of work, and make sure they get the best services out of these people.

The largest organisations need this in order to succeed. When looking at your small business, you need to have a big-business mentality. In other words, you need to look at where all the advantages are you could obtain by having amazing people around you who provide services that are not within your area of expertise.

This gives you more time to do what you are good at. It is also the effect of being a true leader in your business.

One day, I was working with a consultant who had just spent the last three days going through all her accounts for the previous month. She was doing her bookkeeping work. Not only was it draining her, it took her away from her core business. I was curious, and asked her why she was doing it.

She said, "Well, I've got this new software program enables me to use this to manage my accounts." The challenge was because she didn't manage them on a daily it turned into a big project at the end of the month which took up an enormous amount of time.

She had to reschedule some of our client appointments in order to get her bookkeeping done. I said to her, "I have a solution for you. The solution is I'm going to help you get very good at outsourcing."

She was curious and we managed to transform her business in a matter of a few hours. When you outsource, you take out of your business what you are not good at, and you give it to somebody else to do. It's as simple as that.

This has many advantages. Even though those services may cost you a small investment, by giving them to somebody else to do what you by being able to have time to focus on your clients and generate your income is quite profound. The balance is definitely to your advantage.

The other challenge with taking on tasks you're not good at is they often take double, triple, or even days more in time than the person who is the expert at doing them. Typically in a business, I find there are a number of things that can be outsourced to the advantage of the business owner.

- Shop online for your business supplies, you can save hours of running around going to different retailers and buying things you need. The time you save is worth the shipping costs.

- If you have to write long reports, you might want to consider dictation and them transcribed by others. There are terrific online services that enable you to do this.

- Review all of your administration, bookkeeping and accounting tasks. Getting this done by others will save you a lot of time.

What are the areas in your business you could outsource?

The best way for you to determine this is to look at all the tasks you do that are not consulting and are not your core business – in other words, the tasks you do that don't generate any income for you.

Next to those tasks, code them with the level degree of difficulty. Are they something you're good at or you're not good at? Leaders are not good at everything, and what makes them a leader is the ability to recognise this fact, and have the right people around them who are good at doing those things they're not good at. Once you've coded your tasks, look at the areas that could be outsourced. Consider how much time you would save by outsourcing these to other people and how you might be able to organise your business differently, so things could be done on time and with efficiency, by using the services of somebody else.

Determine how much time you will free up by having your difficult non-income generating tasks outsourced to others. You will reallocate this time back to recreation and lifestyle activities or to clients.

Once you've done this, ask trusted friends and colleagues who they use for the various services you need. Interview the people, ensure you are with the right suppliers, and immediately start outsourcing these services to others. Lastly, monitor them to make sure your deadlines are achieved.

This will be liberating for your business. There is no reason for you to do tasks that you're not good at. They simply take your focus away from what you should be doing, which is to look after your clients and have plenty of time to do all of the activities that energise you and make you feel good in business.

Outsourcing changed the life of my client. She was able to save an entire day a week per month, and was able to see more clients. She now stops having to reschedule clients around her bookkeeping and other tasks that clearly took up a lot of time because they were not her core area of expertise.

The amount of time you could save by outsourcing tasks is surprising when you sit down and look at it. I suggest you do this, because it is a terrific way in which you can become more efficient, increase your income, and increase your leisure time, whilst reducing your stress levels in business.

CHAPTER 24
LIFE BALANCE
ESSENTIALS

When you work in your own business and as a consultant, your life balance essentials are driven by you and what you choose to do. This is very different to an employment situation where you have 9:00 to 5:00 or set working hours. You need to be very much in control of how you look after your lifestyle and how you look after your health.

Your ability to perform at a high level on a continual basis in your own business is going to be determined by your life balance essentials. There are certain things you can look out for in doing this.

Often I work with business people and practitioners who don't have their life balance essentials sorted. As a consequence, they find they become very tired and get burnt out quickly. I believe this contributes to premature aging and negative health outcomes.

While there are some great advantages of being in your own business in terms of flexibility, there are also some significant disadvantages if you are not getting your life balance essentials right. There are a number of things you can do in order to make sure this works for you.

The first is to know absolutely and categorically what you do for a living and how you do it. It's really important for you to be able to define this and have absolute clarity on what you do. Believe me, it can be very draining when you are a consultant or in your own business and you are still trying to work out what you actually do. Make sure your services and your products are very, very clear so when you are promoting them, you know exactly what you're going to tell people.

I find it very interesting to see businesses where there is a lack of growth and actually find out when working with the owner of that business that they are not clear on what it is they do for a living. If you are not clear on what you do for a living, how can any of your clients or the market be clear on what you are doing? If that's the circumstance, how are other people going to promote your goods and services if you yourself have no idea what it is you're up to? It can be extremely draining for you if you don't define this early.

The next life balance essential is to make sure you move your body. So much of what we do today, particularly in consulting, can be sedentary. It's important to continually move your body. Ninety percent of brain stimulation comes from the moving of the spine. Recently, Nobel Prize-winner Dr. Roger Sperry talked about this and about the importance of nervous system health in brain functioning and general health.

If you think about the fact that most people are sedentary these days, you will appreciate that brain stimulation simply isn't happening. When you move your body and you stimulate your brain, it has a profound effect on your health. It helps you with stress levels and it helps your body to function at an optimal level.

Your nervous system is the bossiest system in your body. It controls every function. It is very important for your health to be conscious that you move regularly to provide your body with the resources to function at an optimal level.

So many people I work with are very drained and tired. What I find is that they're not moving their body enough and so their nervous system is not getting the stimulation it needs. As a consequence, their brain function is not great and they find they have brain-fog, and get tired and drained easily. This can make them think they're in the wrong career or they should have made different choices in business. This is not the truth. The truth is they need to move their body in order to function at a high level and when they do that, everything else becomes easier for them.

The next life balance essential is to look after your body in terms of fresh food. My suggestion is to have a 70 percent fresh food diet. Also give your body the hydration it needs. You are 70 percent water. If you work with people all day and you fail to drink enough water, you will get tired.

Do this over a number of years and your burnout rate is extremely fast. While you may be OK for the first few clients in the morning, by the time you get to the afternoon, you're dizzy and you can't see straight. Consequently, your body is dehydrated and for long-term health outcomes this can be a high risk for you in business.

It's really important to get the hydration you need. You can achieve this by drinking lots of water, and make your diet 70 percent fresh food. This gives your brain the resources to operate at the highest level and you can give exceptional service to your clients because you are functioning optimally.

The next life balance essential is to have an affirmation; to have something you actually stand for that you share every day that's really important to you. I have a number of affirmations, but one of my favourites in business is this: "I am of service and everything I want and need comes to me easily and effortlessly now."

This is something I say to myself every morning when I wake up; often when I look at myself in a mirror; and definitely while I drive to work. It's really important to know what you stand for and what's important for you. I think your affirmation, said in the present tense, will keep you on the right track for achieving the life you want.

The next step is to set goals, and after you've set your goals remember that goals are a team sport. In my first book, I talk about how to set goals and the fact it's important to appreciate when you want to achieve a goal you need to bring the right people around you in order to do that.

I talk about working on the Olympic Games and how my experience at the Games taught me that goals are only scored in team sport. In other words, the individual sports in the Olympic Games are not goal driven. But when you get a team together, many sports have a goal as their final outcome. In other words, there's hockey and there's football and there's other sports that require goal setting and goal scoring in order for the achievement to happen.

In individual sports, people don't score goals. In team sports, they do. I like to use that as an important metaphor for what you need to do in your life for life balance essentials. Once you've set your goals, work out who in your life or who you could bring into your life is actually going to help you to achieve them. Remember that your goal will be scored when you bring the right people around you.

The next life balance essential is to think counter intuitively. Every time a problem comes up in your business, you need to think about how you could solve it in a different way. What would be the opposite thinking? This is what I do in my business all the time. I find it gives me breakthroughs so much faster and with much better clarity and phenomenal outcomes which I thought I couldn't achieve.

In everything, look at it from different angles and see how you can step out of it, observe it and then create what you want instead. I find that thinking counter intuitively deliberately in business is very important for my success. I believe it's also important for life balance. You see, when you're not thinking counter intuitively, it's very easy to get caught up in a lot of drama. When you're caught in drama, it can be very draining; deplete your energy and focus; and make your business difficult to run.

The next life balance essential is to get plenty of sleep. Make sure this is quality sleep as well. Set up your sleep environment properly without any technology so you can actually have a restful night sleep.

There are a number of things I do for this in my house. I use "Safe Space" technology which looks after the energy around us. I have these devices located in my home in order to reduce the amount of electro-magnetic radiation that impacts me and my family at night.

I'm so keen on this technology I've invested in a business that is developing technology to protect people from the effects of electro-magnetic radiation. I feel this is completely underestimated. If you want to get your life balance essentials right, you need to look at these systems and have them in your home. It can be simple to install and it is quite interesting to see the benefits when you get quality sleep.

Another life balance essential I think is very important is to have a media fast. I regularly go on a media fast, where I don't look at the news or the newspaper for a couple of days at a time. I find this is an important way of me being able to get the space and mental clarity I need without worrying about the drama that's happening in the world at the time.

Sometimes, I'll do this for several weeks at a time. Believe me, there's enough that I hear on the streets that lets me know what's happening in the news and what's really important. I find getting bogged down in a lot of media is not helpful. If the apocalypse happens, I assure you I will know about it by what's happening in the world and people around me. I don't need to be wasting my time engaging with it all the time by going onto the Internet and watching television.

When I did my first media fast, I thought I would find it very difficult and I would feel out of touch. The exact opposite happened. I felt more in touch because I was not concerned about things that were not impacting me. This enabled me to focus on what was truly important in my local community, my family, my business, and with my clients. This is my most important focus and this is the area where I can have the greatest level of influence.

Part of my life balance essentials is to focus on what it is I can influence. I have cut out a lot of media by only watching and being interested in something I can truly impact.

The next life balance essential is to make sure you check in with what's happening in your life and you ask yourself regularly, in fact, many times a day, "Does this energise me or does this drain me?" To operate at a high vibration, you need to be clear about what brings energy into your life and what drains you. I find this is an important part of creating life balance essentials and maintaining my health.

When you've determined what energises you, focus on those tasks. When you've determined what drains you, work out how you're going to extract those events or those activities from your life. You can always outsource them or give them to other people. If you can't outsource the task, change your mindset about it.

The most important thing you are doing here is to put yourself in an environment where you feel energised. When you do that, you can work at peak performance and deliver outstanding results to your clients. More importantly, you're also caring for your own health while you are do this because you reduce your stress levels considerably by only working on things that bring you energy.

It's very important you pay yourself first and as you are advised in the safety demonstration on a commercial airline flight, put on your own oxygen mask before assisting others.

Another life balance essential is to move forward in the midst of change and not revert to old habit patterns. In leadership there will be times of human upset, especially as you transform and live in a place of authenticity. There will be people who find your new assertiveness challenges their ability to achieve their own outcomes. In the past, you may have accepted circumstances that drained you and were poor choices for creating your best life. Now as the observer, you may see that you accepted people in your life who have blocked your success. You may have allowed this for years and even decades. To recognise and appreciate the events that now enable you to see these people isn't easy. It's time to stay in your light and allow these people and situations to move away. To experience these events without reverting back to old ways is an essential part of transformative leadership and it transforms how you live in all areas of your life.

Take the word "live." Remove the "i" because it may keep you from moving ahead and with your new found resources add an element of surprising yourself with capabilities you know you can use every day. This gives you an "oh!" element of surprise in the greatness that is you. Add the "o" into "l-ve" where you removed the "i" and in this moment you have learnt to "love" who you are and what you stand for. Rather than simply "live" with and accept something you know you want to change for a greater good.

The last life balance essential is something my late father taught me. He said to me that in business the most important thing you can do is to pay yourself first and look after your own needs before you look after the needs of others. Often when I'm flying, my father will come into my mind when they give the safety demonstration and they say to us we must put on our own oxygen mask before assisting others. This reminds me of my father who was always of the belief that you must look after yourself first and then you look after others.

Having your life balance essentials right in business is a vital key to your success. When you're employed, you generally have set hours and your commitment is to somebody else. But when you're in business, you need to be vigilant about what you do to maintain your own success and health along the way. No one is going to be there for you telling you what to do. You must take care of this yourself.

CHAPTER 25
BEST CLIENTS ONLY

D o you ever see somebody's name in your schedule or think about a client and suddenly have a feeling of dread? I hear all the time from consultants that they have clients who drain them and they don't like working with. In this chapter, I show you how to choose the best clients for your business and make sure you only work with the people who uplift your energy.

What's important to understand is we have become a global community and people have lots of choice. In your business, you get to choose your clients. They don't choose you. It's important for you to match what you do and what energises you with the people who come to you for help.

You need to be discerning and disciplined with this. There's no point taking everybody just because you feel you need the business. To have a client who drains you is far worse for your business than to have no client at all. It's important for you to determine what your best clients look like and make a commitment to only choose these clients for your business.

I was working with a chiropractor and the number of patients she saw was dwindling. Her business was rapidly going backwards. I said to her, "Would you like to sit down and go through your list of clients? And let's have a look and see who they are and where you're up to with their care programs."

As we started to go through her list, I could see she had attracted a lot of people who drained her. The challenge was she hadn't stepped into her leadership role, and so she allowed them to determine the course of their care rather than being the specialist who showed her client where they needed to go with their care.

A number of her clients were dropping out of care or coming in just when they felt like it and she wasn't getting results with them. This was draining her. She felt really beaten up by it and was concerned about where her business was heading.

We decided to create what it would take for someone to be a "best client only" and then work backwards through her list of patients to see who the best clients were within it.

What we determined was that there were a number of clients who didn't follow the care protocols and she had been unable to get through to them what they really needed.

I explained to her that this mismatch is actually OK. There's nothing wrong with it. The only problem is not allowing those clients to move on to something else when it has been determined they're not willing to follow the program she set for them.

The most important thing you need to do to create a culture of "best clients" is to take the leadership role right from the beginning. Earlier in this book, you read about how to be a leader in your business. If you are not the leader with your clients, you will struggle to determine whether they're good clients for you or not. When you aren't in the leadership role, no client will uplift your energy because you're not taking them on the journey they need to go on and you're not being the leader they need you to be.

Once you've decided what you're doing in terms of leading your clients, you need to stay true to this and listen for the signs. If a client does not comply with what you require of them or what you know to be good for them in terms of getting the outcomes they want, you need to have enough courage to say you can no longer help them.

This is a key element of being a leader in business. It also involves ethics. There's no point in you taking fees from people who you are not helping. If a client is not willing to follow the program with you, then how are you supposed to help them?

I remember hearing a story many years ago and it's quite a sad story about a woman in New Zealand. She'd been to see a specialist. This specialist was going to help her with her cancer diagnosis. The specialist recommended some radical treatment for her. She only wanted to take on half of his recommendations.

When she went back to the specialist to say, "Look, I'm prepared to do this part of your recommendation, but not these parts," the specialist turned around and said to her, "I'm very sorry, but I can't help you. I can only help you with the full recommendation of everything I've suggested. Otherwise I'm not prepared to take your money to only give you half of what I have suggested here. My role is to use my knowledge to save your life and that's what I intend to do. But if you only want half of that, I won't take any of your money and I would be happy to refer you to somebody else if that would be helpful for you."

She decided not to have the care of that doctor and instead go and do her own thing with somebody else. She had another doctor she was happy to work with. This doctor was happy to accept her terms, which was that she only wanted to do half the treatment that had been recommended to save her life. Unfortunately, this woman passed away within 12 months. She had curable cancer.

What I find so interesting about this story is the doctor's conviction in making sure he only took on his best clients. In other words, he was unwilling to take any client who was not prepared to take on the entire program.

He definitely could not guarantee outcomes for any patient, but what he knew to be true was that certain protocols needed to be put in place for him to have the best opportunity to save that client's life.

He didn't take it personally that that client only wanted half of his service. What he did do was he stood by what he knew to be true and he allowed that client to go somewhere else and said to that client he would not treat them with only half the protocol. I think this is an awesome lesson in making sure you really create the best outcomes for your clients.

When I spoke to the doctor about what he had done in this circumstance, he said to me, "If a client only wants to take on half of my care recommendations, it can be very draining for me because I'm in the business of saving people's lives. If somebody comes to me and wants their life to be saved, I'm going to do everything possible to make that happen. If I agree early in the piece to only do half of my job, then what outcome am I going to achieve for them? I'm going to be sad and frustrated and think about that patient every night of the week, wondering whether they're going to survive or not and know that I'm only doing half of my job for them. I'm not prepared to live with this."

I thought what a phenomenal response he had in standing in his leadership. What do you need to do in order to make sure you get this right in your business? First of all, I reiterate, you need to be in leadership from the very beginning. You need to be able to work out whether a client is actually following your protocol or not.

If they're not following your protocol, sit down with them and seek to understand. The process of seeking to understand is something I detail in my first book, "The Lateral Thinking Entrepreneur: 33 Principals for Expansive Leadership." To understand means to interpret or view something in a particular way. Behaviour means the way in which someone acts or conducts themselves. What is involved in understanding behaviour is to consider 'what' and 'how' life experiences, beliefs, values, family of origin, geography, religion, education, state of health are "impacting" how your client views the protocol and determines whether the manner in which work with them is a good match for how they learn, achieve and measure their own success. An opinion and a belief is neither right nor wrong, it "just is" based on the person who has formed it. Your role is to find the conditions that are limitations in the way you are interacting with your client and then discover the way your client could better receive information, education or your insights specific to their model of the world. Anything less than this level of commitment means your client needs more information from you to be committed.

Once you have done this, if the client is still not willing to follow your care protocol or your recommendations, you need to look at whether you're willing to continue to look after them.

I don't believe there are any positive outcomes in taking fees from people who you seriously cannot help. If you know a protocol needs to be followed and isn't being followed, why would you want to continue to help that person if you think you're going to fail them?

After you've had the honest conversation with your client, if they are still unwilling to follow the protocol you recommend for them, it's important you let them go. Let them go somewhere else where they will be able to get the service they want.

This is not about you bending to comply with what they want in this circumstance. It's about you standing in your power as a leader and knowing in your professional and expert wisdom what you believe that client needs. You don't always get this right and that's not the point. The point is to be congruent in your leadership role.

Back to my chiropractor. We realised that a number of her patients were dropping out of care because they were not following the protocol. Much to her horror, I suggested to her she contact those clients and tell them she could no longer care for them. She was really upset because she thought this would destroy her business, but she was willing to give it a go.

We worked out some scripts and things to say to those clients in order to let them go in a way that was fair and ethical and to give them the opportunity to continue with care if they were willing to do it on the terms she needed for them to get the results.

Some of the clients decided to schedule their appointments properly and look after their health in the way she recommended. Others decided they would rather go elsewhere. As a consequence of this, the energy in her business completely changed.

At the time I worked with her, her number had gone down to 30 client visits a week. When we checked in again five weeks later, she had seen 70 clients that week. She had let go of a few patients and made space for new people to come in.

More importantly, she had stepped into her power as a leader to find her best clients only. She made sure she kept only the clients that were willing to follow her protocol.

When you work with your best clients on your programs you will always feel energised because you know what it takes for them to get results. The minute you start to feel drained, you need to reflect on whether that client is following your recommendations or not.

If they are not following your recommendations have the courage to let them go. There are so many people out there you can help. You need to be able to help them though with what you know as a professional and leader to be the right process for them to participate in.

They've come to you because they want to be helped with something they otherwise could not do on their own. Your ability to stand in the power of this is very important.

Once you work out how to do this in your business, you have a terrific advantage to ensure that everyone you work with energises you and gets the results you so want them to get.

There will still be some people who will follow the protocols you recommend and may not get the results. You have two options – refer these people to another practitioner or you reassess and review their case as suggested in Chapter 10 Client Reviews in order to make sure you keep them on track.

To have your best clients you need to ensure you have a high energy level all the time and that you are able to deliver the best results. This can be absolutely fantastic for your business success and I highly recommend it.

CHAPTER 26
99%

O ver my many years in business, I've come to realise something that was very confronting when I first started to deal with it. I hear all the time from my clients that they're looking for consistency in what they do, and they will often turn around and say to me, "I just need to be consistent."

The challenge with this is they're aiming for 99 percent. I find this very difficult to achieve in my own life, and so what I share with them is that 99 percent is not easy at all. Often people are very perplexed by this, but let me share with you what it is I think is so much easier to achieve.

In life, if we decide to do something 99 percent of the time, there's always a risk we won't do it and we won't do it at all. To me, 99 percent means either 99 percent or not at all, which means that the risk of not doing it is very high.

A number of years ago, I found my work / life balance was quite challenging and my goals were not being achieved as fast as I wanted. I determined that there were a number of things I was prepared to be 99 percent committed to.

I realised this wasn't helping me. Instead I created a list of all the things I was 100 percent committed to. By being 100 percent committed to them, I was always going to do the tasks it took in order to get these things done without there being any shadow of a doubt as to whether I would do it or not. This completely transformed my business.

100 percent means completion. It means that everything is finished. 99 percent means you could take it or leave it, and it actually sets you up to fail. In your business and in your life, it's important to determine the things you are absolutely committed to, and to sit with these things and do them on a daily basis, with absolute clarity of knowing you will do them no matter what.

There are lots of things in your life you will find you are already 100 percent committed to. They might be simple things, like getting up in the morning and brushing your teeth, or having one coffee on the way to work. These are the things that you do 100 percent of the time.

In business and in life, it's important to expand on this and determine what things are really important for your success. These things need to become the not-negotiables that you will do 100 percent of the time. Knowing the outcome you will achieve is a consequence of this and is exactly what you're looking for.

The first step to determine this is to identify the tasks that energise you and the tasks that drain you in your business. What are the things you try to be consistent with? This will give you a good idea as to whether you're 100 percent committed or not.

Then sit down and have an honest look at what these things are costing you. Sometimes the cost will be very low. Other times, the cost will be very high. If the cost of trying to do something 99 percent of the time instead of committing to do it 100 percent of the time is high, then you need to rethink how you're going to manage this.

It may be that you decide you just don't want to do that task at all. That's fine. Just get rid of it, so you're not beating yourself up about it when you don't achieve it.

If instead you'd like to be 100 percent committed to it, sit down and work out how this will be possible and implement so there is no negotiation and you will do it 100 percent of the time.

It's very important to get rid of all the 99-percent-or-less items in your life cause you to be held back in what you really want to achieve. You'll find by committing to fewer things, but making those commitments 100 percent, you get a far better result than having a number of things you are willing to commit to 99 percent of the time, and spend the rest of the time stressed when you don't do it.

I've found this to be quite transformative in business.

CHAPTER 27
THE GIFT OF STORYTELLING

D o you sometimes get the feeling you are lecturing your clients and it feels really uncomfortable? Sometimes we have so much we want to share with the people we're working with to help them get the results, that by telling them directly they seem to shut down and not listen at all?

This can be really frustrating. If you have ever experienced this, you are going to love this chapter where I share with you how to become an amazing storyteller and how storytelling will transform your business.

When you tell a story, what you are doing is using metaphor. Metaphors are words and phrases that are literally not applicable to what you're talking about. It's more of a figure of speech, an analogy, or a comparison enabling somebody to understand what it is you are trying to tell them, but by way of telling somebody else's story.

By finding these parallel stories, you can help your clients by taking them on a journey of where you would like them to go with their own results, but by using somebody else's story as the best way to exemplify the journey they are about to go on.

Over the years, I have become a real fan of storytelling, because it has had a profound impact on the success I've had and also that of my clients.

What you often find with people is they really don't want to be lectured at. They don't want to be told the things they're doing aren't right. It can be very difficult for somebody to accept your suggestions to them when they feel they're directed specifically to them and there's no context for the fact that just like other people, they have similar issues.

When somebody believes their problem is something experienced by other people and there are solutions for that – and you can share this in story format with them -- you will find their ability to replicate the process is far easier and they feel happier about the journey they're about to go on.

When you work with clients, in many situations you find there is a specific way in which they will present themselves to you when they first come in. Generally, they have a problem that's led to a crisis and with this they need resources in order to achieve their outcome.

Later I will explain this to you in more detail. But right now I'm explaining to you how to use those four steps in terms of becoming a great storyteller. When a client comes to you with a problem, it's important for you to think laterally and think about other examples in your business where you've dealt with similar circumstances and taken your client on a journey.

There's no need to use names or identify people. You want to keep your clients' identities private, but you do want to share their stories.

It's important for you to do that.

The best way to do it is to start off with, "One day I had..." and then go on to tell the story that is a parallel. You want to start with the problem that was presented with the other client, how that problem turned into a crisis, what the resources were that were applied to it, and ultimately, what the victory was at the end and how that person resolved it.

When you become terrific at storytelling, you can find you will communicate all the information you need to give to your clients in a manner that helps them and their non-conscious brain to process the journey they're about to go on.

It's true leadership when you can use metaphors and stories with your clients to be able to take them on a journey where they need to go in order to get their ultimate outcome.

Sometimes people find when they're sitting down and being told the journey they're about to go on, without the context of somebody else who's gone before them and achieved the outcomes they're looking for, it can be difficult for them to feel convinced they will get the outcome they seek.

When you share the journey in story form by creating an analogy and a parallel, people are a lot more receptive to what it is you want to share with them. My suggestion is you become very good at story-telling. You will find in your business that there are lots of parallel situations that keep presenting time and time again.

Choose your best stories of this, and make sure you share them regularly with your clients so they get the parallel experience and their non-conscious brain opens up to the possibilities that are open to them through the stories of others.

Often people can have the feeling when they're working with you that perhaps you don't understand their problem.

By not making it about the client and instead making it about the story you show them by example that you have achieved the outcome with somebody else. You helped them on their journey and you will help your client feel understood in a way that gives them confidence in your ability to help them succeed.

This is an incredibly powerful resource you can use in your business.

CHAPTER 28
SOCIAL MEDIA

Something my clients often ask me is what to do about social media. I hear it takes a long time for people to get their social media right. They seem to be spending a lot of time on it without knowing whether they're truly getting a result.

In this chapter, I share with you my thoughts on social media and how it can be used to your advantage. Some of my thoughts about this are quite controversial. I believe social media is a platform for you to stand in your power and to let people know who you are.

What to avoid with social media is using it as a platform to sell your products and services directly. I really don't believe it's designed for that, instead I think it's designed to create rapport to enable people to see you as a human being, and to see who you really are and what you stand for.

I find businesses that continually try to sell their services through social media are really annoying. I tend to unfollow them or stop their feeds because I'm not interested in having this information thrown at me the whole time.

Here are some of my tips for social media:

- The first is to follow your tribe. I find social media isn't just about what you post, but it's about what you read as well. I'm very inspired by following people who I think are good business people and who have the same kind of beliefs and values as me. I look for the people who I consider to be in my tribe and who I want to learn from. I make a point of following these people every day. I choose the people who inspire me with messages, and inspire me because they've been successful in the industries I work in. I am determined to always follow my tribe and be inspired by them.

- The next thing I do is look at what gets noticed by other people. I'm fascinated to see how many shares and likes are being attributed to certain things that are posted on social media. I'm looking for a trend. What you need to do is start looking behind what's posted and behind what gets a whole lot of likes or shares, and trends virally, to see what the best solutions are in terms of the content people are looking for. When you do this, it's quite surprising to see what people share and what people like content-wise. It's very important to have a really good understanding of what other people notice. Don't just look at it from the point of view of the content, but look at it from behind the content. In other words, what is it people achieve from this? Is it inspiring them? Motivating them? Making them feel happier? Assisting them in their success? Bringing out the best in others? What is it about that content that makes people like it and makes people want to share it? You want to create the parallel experience with what you're sharing, and the best way to do this is to look at and examine what other people are doing.

- Next you want to be visual. When people go through social media pictures have more impact. So it's important you use more pictures and limit the words in your posts unless you have an important message. With my business social media pages, when we post photographs we often get more attention than if we simply post a few words. It's important to look at your social media from the point of view of a picture is worth a thousand words. Look for ways to use images in the place of words.

- Be sure your content is always personal, uplifting, inspiring and motivational. It's important for you to set a high vibration for everything you do. If your social media account slides into complaining about things or operates at a low vibration, this is negative for your business. Always look to inspire and motivate people. Share things you think will be helpful for people to achieve even more success in their life. Have a huge amount of generosity around this.

- The next is to use social media for gratitude. I think gratitude is actually medicine, and the more you can use your social media to show you are a person of immense gratitude, the more other people will be attracted to you and your clients.

- Look at frequency. Be consistent with the content you post and the frequency with which you post it. If you're going to decide to work in a social media context, you need to be able to have a consistent profile of what you do. Set a schedule of what it is you're going to post and when you're going to post it, and do this consistently. Your clients and people who follow you will look for consistency in what you do, because this says a lot about you and who you are in business.

- Next you need to decide on your personal messages and stay in theme. Make sure your personal messages are very congruent with what you believe the world needs and what your clients most like about you. Stay really consistent with this. Your personal message is a part of your leadership blueprint. It's really important for you to own this and to feel really confident about how you share this with other people. This is what you stand for and your contribution to the world.

- Choose to be a resource. Connect people, post other people's content, refer to other people who you feel are professional and very good in their field, and be a resource for other people. This is a terrific way of using social media.

- Above all, never use social media to sell. Social media is about creating a framework around you that attracts people to you. Once they've come to you, then you have an opportunity to sell your services.

I believe social media is about being social! It's about interacting with other people. When you are interacting with other people, the most important thing you need to do is make sure they know what you value. What motivates you, what inspires you, what you are willing to share and what you are willing to give?

I don't feel social media is a platform for selling anything. Take these tips into your social media and see how it transforms your business.

CHAPTER 29
YOUR GUIDE TO TAKING A HOLIDAY

I'm amazed at the number of clients I mentor who never take a holiday. This really bothers me, because I feel, "Why are you working unless you actually have some quality recreation time for yourself?"

The challenge when you work in your own business is you tend to feel that taking a holiday is going to have a significant impact on your earnings. I hear this all the time and it prevents people from having the holidays they need and deserve.

In this chapter, I show you the easiest and most effective ways to take a holiday without it having a negative impact on your finances and your earnings. Many years ago, I decided I would create my own system of taking holidays every year. Every three months, I schedule one week off and cross it out in my diary from the very beginning of the year. I don't always get to plan my holidays in terms of what I want to do activity-wise, but I do always have that week off from the beginning of the year.

When I take a holiday or a break, I make a point of planning the activity for the next holiday on my way home. I decide what I going to do next and I book it at least three months in advance and sometimes more. This is a terrific way for me to always have something to look forward that gives me the life balance I need.

The reason to have regular holidays is because it is important for your health and your success. I find after most people book regular holidays they see no change in their income. In fact, they actually see it go up. You see, people are energy, and when you get tired, you're unable to function at the same level as when you're feeling refreshed.

If you are not taking a regular break, then you will find you get tired more quickly, and it becomes difficult for you to maintain a high level of engagement with your clients the whole time. When you take a regular break and refresh yourself, you get a new perspective. When you come back to work, you are more productive than when you left.

The important thing is to schedule it. Here's how I organize that I take a quality break of at least one week every three months. The first thing I do is pre-schedule the whole year. In other words, I will decide which of the four weeks I'm going to take off and when they're going to be.

I cross these dates off in my diary from the very beginning of the year. I like to take at least one week off every three months. By scheduling it at the beginning of the year, it makes absolutely no impact on my clients or my business when this is done in advance.

The next thing you need to do is set aside at least five percent, but preferably seven percent, of your weekly income into a holiday fund. Just pop it across into another account. When you are employed and earning a salary, your employer will be putting aside money every week for you for holiday pay.

In small business, we tend not to do this. We keep going along and forget about the fact we need a holiday one day. When you set aside the money every week toward your holiday fund, you still have earnings while you are on holiday. This is an important part of managing your business successfully.

After you've crossed out your diary, you need to make sure your clients become aware of when you are taking breaks. The next step is to create some urgency before you go. There are some terrific ways I use in my business when my practitioners take holidays. I also recommend this to my mentoring clients too, as most find they get an enormous level of success and engagement from it.

In the months leading up to your holidays, let your clients know you'll be going away for a week. Use this as an opportunity to pre-schedule them. The scarcity mindset of you being away and unable to service them means they will pre-book their appointments, not wanting to miss out. This is really important.

In my businesses, about three weeks out from a key staff member taking leave, we contact clients to let them know their preferred consultant is going away. This has a profound impact. People contact us immediately to book in for an appointment feeling they need some care and use this as an opportunity to come in before the consultant is away.

People often get upset when their practitioner or consultant of choice is away on holiday and they call for an appointment and cannot get in because they are not there. It's so much better and nicer courtesy for your clients if you tell them in advance you are going away and give them the opportunity to book in before you go.

The next thing we do is send a holiday postcard. This is a terrific marketing opportunity. If you go back and review the chapter on postcards, you will see what the steps are in order to do this. People love receiving postcards, and it doesn't matter whether you're taking a week off to go to a conference or you're having a vacation or even a staycation.

Setting up your marketing in a way that sends a message to all your clients in the form of a postcard is a terrific marketing tool and a great way of keeping in touch with them. It's a simplified way of people having an insight into what's going on in your life. So make sure you share with them what you are up to.

Of course, there may be some professions in which this is just not OK to do. But for the most part, it's a terrific way of marketing to people and letting them know you're away, that you want to have a bit of fun, and you are sharing something with them that is a little bit left of field. People will always appreciate it. I'm always amazed at how many people contact me after sending holiday postcards to say, "Thanks for the postcard."

The next step is to contact your clients again when you get back. It's important when you get back from your break to send an SMS message to your clients or just get in contact with them to let them know you're back and they can re-engage with your services.

What you will find, by pre-scheduling your vacations four times a year, and by making sure you use these strategies around marketing when it comes to holidays, is they make absolutely no impact on your business. In other words, there is no loss of income for the fact you are taking time off. The main reason many small business people don't take proper breaks is because they simply fail to plan. When people take advantage of setting up their breaks in a proper manner, as I have shared with you, their income goes up, their energy levels go up, and their ability to engage more clients increases, because people feel refreshed after having a break.

There is no excuse for failing to take a holiday. No one is going to offer you holidays unless you set it up for yourself. If you have decided to be a success in small business, you need to create the right environment for you to have a holiday.

CHAPTER 30
FLEXIBILITY IS CONTROL

When I think about the importance of behavioural flexibility in business, I often think about a big tree on a stormy day. What is it about the tree that enables it to survive the storm? Well, their roots are firmly planted in the ground yet they're able to move with the winds and the storm in a way that enables them to stay upright.

I consider this to be an important ability in business, and especially when you're working with other people. I find the highest level of flexibility gives you the highest level of control in your business relationships.

The advantage of making sure you have a flexible approach in what you do is that you can maintain your energy levels at a high state. You can find the easiest pathways to success and be of service to other people. You maintain your independence and flow in what you do, without being caught up in other people's drama.

When I mentor clients their ability to understand that flexibility equals control is paramount to their success. If you can bend and not break, you have a great ingredient for your business success. What you need to appreciate is that, however anyone shows up to you, you have the ability to deal with it.

Behavioural flexibility refers to being able to be adaptive to changes in the external or internal environment. This means you need to always be logical-levels above of the people you deal with.

Many years ago I was witness to an accident. In seeing how the paramedics dealt with this enabled me to understand how important behavioural flexibility is. When a paramedic turns up to the scene of an accident, often they have no idea what they're about to deal with.

Their ability to gain control of the situation is dependent on their flexibility in how they handle every single thing that comes up. You don't see a paramedic getting involved in the drama while they're trying to help people. They observe the situation and then take the necessary action to make sure everybody is safe.

Watching this made me appreciate that this is something I do every day in business. I create environments where I observe what's going on, and then have the behavioural flexibility to create the outcome I want. This ultimately gives me a high level of control in what I do.

These are the steps I take in order to have flexibility and control. The first thing is, like the big tree in the storm, I always make sure I'm grounded. In other words, I know exactly what I am doing and how I am going to do it. I stand in the power of this as a leader.

If you are feeling uncertain or unsure, it's very difficult for you to have a high level of behavioural flexibility because you are always going to feel as though you are under attack.

The next thing I do is work out what needs to be returned to sender.

This may sound weird, but it's very important you appreciate that people will often dump things on you that don't belong to you.

If somebody's behaviour toward you is a reflection of what's going on with them, and they're merely projecting it toward you. To my mind, you need to be able to turn around and say, "That isn't my stuff and I need to return it to sender."

Behavioural flexibility is not about allowing other people to walk all over you. It's about being logical-levels above, and knowing what you own and the journey that you need to take people on. Making sure that you're able to lead with certainty and in an ethical way.

The next step is when it comes to drama you are always the observer and the creator. When you have a flexible level of behaviour and deal with clients, you need to appreciate that people will come to you with drama.

Your ability to just see that for what it is and take the client on the journey they need to go on is very important for your success and theirs. If you get into their drama and become a part of it, you will have no control over the outcome.

If you would like more information on this, I suggest review the chapter on Drama in my book "The Lateral-Thinking Entrepreneur: 33 Principles of Expansive Leadership". You need to show leadership all the time. What I mean by that is you need to assert where you're up to with your clients and that you intend to take a leadership journey with them.

If you review Chapter 25 Best Clients Only, you will understand that in order for you to create the best environment for your clients to thrive, you need to be able to pick and choose who you work with. Your behavioural flexibility with this is paramount to your success.

It may seem counterintuitive that flexibility is very important in business and it gives you an ultimate level of control. Yet this has been one of the key success factors in my businesses for the last 25 years.

Back to the paramedics at the accident. They managed to get control of the entire situation very quickly. There were people who were injured, people who were stressed, and people who were going berserk. Yet they managed to use their flexibility to create the ultimate level of control. This gave everybody certainty that the outcome was going to be OK.

Observing this, I was absolutely amazed at the pace in which they managed to resolve everything that was going on and bring everyone to safety. This taught me an enormous lesson about the importance of flexibility in business. How having the highest level of flexibility and being able to deal with anything when it shows up, ultimately gives you the highest level of control.

CHAPTER 31
HOW TO TRULY GROW

H ow do you know if you're actually doing well in business? This is something I'm asked all the time. Sometimes it can be very difficult to predict, particularly when you have your head down and you're simply trying to get on with it.

The challenge is you need to have markers in place that enable you to understand whether you are growing or not. There are a number of things you can do to focus on continually growing your business.

What's most important thing about this is to measure the actions as well as the outcomes, because sometimes, just by undertaking the actions, you get surprising results in a different space of time.

I once had an interesting experience of this with a real estate investment. I stretched myself in order to purchase a property and I was concerned about paying the mortgage off and being able to have more equity in it. Approximately 12 months after purchase, I had a valuer give me a re-assessment on the property's value. Quite surprisingly, it had increased in value significantly and to a far greater extent than I had thought. My entire focus was to pay down the mortgage as quickly as possible, but I didn't realise the energy and focus I put into doing this was being offset at the same time by the increases in value in the market.

Now I appreciate this is not always the way things go with an investment, however, my intention was to grow my business and pay that property off. I realised things are not always what they seem. When you set the right intention, you set in place the things you need to do on a continual basis to create the energy around what you need for your success. It may manifest in surprising ways.

There are a number of things I do to continually grow in business. Here are my top 10:

1. **Educate yourself continuously.** Not a year goes by where I don't attend another course, read more information, or learn something. It's important to continue educating yourself to be successful in your career and business.

2. **Get your mindset right.** Make sure you look after having a healthy mindset and be in the physiology of leader in all areas of your business and in your life. It's amazing how much your mindset impacts your success. By continually doing the things you know get your mindset right, you can have more success than you have ever imagined. Sometimes getting your mindset right is about your nutrition, your exercise, your lifestyle choices, the things you read, meditation, and the people you hang out with. Believe it or not, you can get some inspiring mindset content just by hanging around the right people who are moving forward in their life. If you find you're with people who drain you, then these people will be impact your mindset. Move on or small

doses.

3. **Increase your prices every year.** An important part of your success and growth in business is about increasing your prices. Often I find small business owners simply don't do this. On an annual basis, you need to increase your prices.

4. **Always ask for referrals.** Look at the times where people are truly appreciating you, and consider these referral moments as an opportunity for you to grow your business. For more information on this, review Chapter 11 Referral Moments. This is a critical part of your growth and success.

5. **Give to receive.** It's important for you to always be giving out to other professionals and people who compliment your services in order for you to receive. You need to get the flow of this right in order for it to be successful. Otherwise, you'll just be knocking on doors that will never be opened. Make sure you have a philosophy of giving to receive, of enabling people to have even more success by connecting them with other service providers who can assist them in their journey. For this you will always be rewarded.

6. **Be generous.** Make sure you look at the opportunities you have in simple and easy ways to always be generous and to wow people with VIP service. Look for things you can do that nobody else does, and go the extra mile. This will help you to truly grow your business.

7. **Have a mentor.** Have at least one person who inspires you and has walked the journey you want to walk with the success you want to have. The benefits of a mentor are they have achieved what you want and they have been through the trials and tribulations you may be experiencing. As a consequence, they can save you months and even years of

heartache when you follow their guidance and learn from them. More importantly, learn from the mistakes they made along the way.

8. **Energy is everything.** Money is energy and it takes big energy to make money. Make sure you appreciate what you put into the world is energy and that you get your energy right. Become really attuned to what drains you and what energises you, and make sure you focus on working in the areas that energise you instead of drain you.

9. **Know your goals and review them frequently.** You need to have a map of where you're going and what you want to achieve. It's amazing when I sit down with some books where I've written notes from years back about the goals I set and think about the fact I've not only achieved some of them in remarkable ways, but I've also achieved far beyond those goals. Writing down your goals gives them energy and brings them to life. Once you've written down a goal, you need to take action steps. It's very important you do this, because that's where you get the energy fuel to determine your success, to drive it and achieve it. It's amazing what you can do when you know what your goals are and you know where you are going with them. Make sure you go back and review your goals frequently and continue to check they are fully aligned with where you want to go.

10. **Create systems.** When you create systems in your business, you are defining what you do, and you are simplifying your business in a way that will give you remarkable results. What you measure matters, and by creating the systems that enable you to achieve your ultimate success in the easiest and most straightforward pathway possible, you will ultimately have even greater success in business.

Of course, there has to be a number 11. My number 11 is this. Remember the world is round. For years I have been an incredible advocate for other people's work, and I refer people to other practitioners and other resources all the time. It is something I have become an expert at in my career.

I've often had times where people have contacted me and they've said to me, "Madelaine, for all the referrals you give to us, how can we ever repay you for how much business you have sent to us?"

I have always responded to them in this way. "The world is round. What I do is energetic. While I am giving to you, somebody else is giving to me, and it doesn't work in straight lines. It works in a circle."

While I am out there putting the energy into supporting other businesses and supporting other people who I want to succeed and I want for them to prosper, I myself am receiving the same in return.

The world is round, and what you give, you will receive. This is a philosophy that has been an incredible pathway to my success in business.

CHAPTER 32
DUPLICATING YOURSELF

I am an identical twin, so I've always had a lot of fun with the thought of seeing double. Imagine being able to have the best of you in another person? How might this accelerate your success if you were able to duplicate yourself?

Most business people I work with have started in a situation where they have literally bought themselves a job. In other words, because of their high dependency on trading their time for income without any leverage, they are no better off than being employed by somebody else. Sometimes they are in a more challenging position due to the costs of running a business without leverage of earning beyond hours worked.

Once you've established your independent work situation in a way that gives you a sense of security, it's important to look at how you could duplicate the best of yourself in order to expand and grow into a business that has leverage and has other people delivering results for you.

One of the things very important in how I reverse engineer my business is to look at my opportunities for success through others.

There are some important steps I take in order to achieve this. One of the most important things you want to do is feel you are capable of helping other people achieve success. When you want to leverage your business and create an opportunity to duplicate yourself, it's about you bringing out the best in other people. If you make this your focus, you will find it's a lot easier. The advantages of doing this are that you can leverage your time, increase your success, and create a business instead of a job. When you do this, you find your stress levels go down and you have more free time for yourself.

To duplicate means to make a copy, and when you want to duplicate yourself first know what it is you are duplicating and secondly, make sure you duplicate the best of who you are and what you do. There are a number of things I look at when I think about duplicating myself in business:

Number one, I suggest is that you know your values. What you value are the principles you live by, and you always want these. These are your ethics. Make sure you always work with people who are aligned with your true values. Only this way will you find the best people to work with. There's no right or wrong when it comes to values, so your ability to seek out the people who have similar values to you is very important to your success.

Number two, actively seek to mentor others, and be generous about how you do this. There's no point keeping your information to yourself. If you want to be a change maker and a leader, you have to be active in mentoring other people. This means you can duplicate the best of you in order to be successful. As you help another person, your generosity in doing this will be delivered back to you in your results.

Number three, teach what you do and be prepared to share your knowledge. It's important you have an attitude of bringing people into your business and around you so you can teach them and share your knowledge.

I actively seek to work with a small number of students every year who study business, a healthcare modality, or study in the professions I like to help as a business mentor. This way I can contribute to people before they have started their career. I find it is a terrific way to share my knowledge I know will be of significant impact to other people.

Number four, become an employer. Look at opportunities to employ other people, and create training systems in terms of how you work with these people. You can give them the information and knowledge you want to share with them in order for them to perform at their best.

Number five, be expansive with your people. When you employ staff, look at opportunities to increase what you do and how you deliver your services. One plus one equals eleven when you allow the people you bring into your business to be expansive. Always take them on a journey of authentic change so you can assist them in their career development and, at the same time, bring out the best in them so they will want to be generous with you in terms of what they give to you in your business. This can bring great value to what you do.

Number six, seek people who are coachable. People who are willing to be corrected and guided are coachable. They are usually committed to their own personal and professional development, and they are very hungry for feedback. I actively look at how engaged the people I employ are in self-directed learning. It's important to work with people who are coachable, because you have a far greater chance of success in helping these people to be the best role models in duplicating your success.

Number seven, create your step-by-step. Look at what you do and unpack it. Know how you do what you do and teach this in steps. A lot of people need to know the steps of how to do something. Your ability to bring something down to a step-by-step process will enable you to duplicate yourself with relative ease.

Number eight, document the systems in your business. This way anyone should be able to step into your business at any time and know exactly how you run things. This is an important part of you being able to create the best processes for people to duplicate. When you have documented systems, there's little chance for error. After you have tested the systems, give them to the people who you work with and this will lead to the ultimate successful outcomes you want.

Number nine, have an attitude of abundance. One day I was working with a doctor and he wanted to employ associates in his business. Previously he tried employing associates and had difficulty retaining them. I was curious and wanted to know why this was happening, and he said to me, "What happens is they come in and they steal my clients."

I was really curious about this, and I was thinking, "How can these people possibly be stealing your clients when they're working for you? They're clients of your practice, so how could they be stealing them?"

"Oh no," he exclaimed, "What happens is sometimes I'm not available, and so the patient wants to see the other doctor. Then they see the other doctor, and they want to stay with the other doctor. And I want the patient to stay with me."

I thought about this and thought, "Well, isn't that the point? By you being able to duplicate yourself and have somebody else look after your clients, you actually end up with two things, income and time. How does that sound?"

He found this a very difficult concept to understand, but he realised he was missing the point of duplicating himself. He actually wanted his staff member to be as good and as desired as he was in business, and yet when it actually happened he was calling it stealing patients.

We were able to work through this, and he was able to find a solution that enabled him to be expansive about having an attitude of abundance with his associates.

As a consequence, he was able to hire somebody who was very good and stayed employed by him for many years. He became generous in how he shared his clients and ended up having a lot more time on his hands while still generating income.

Number 10, have a business mentor to help you. When you try to duplicate yourself there is nothing better than having somebody to guide you and help you to create what you want.

A business mentor is somebody who has walked the path you want to walk and has taken the steps you want to take.

The advantage you have by working with a business mentor is the trials and tribulations they have been through become part of something you just need to learn along the way rather than actually having to experience them all yourself.

This can save you years of heartache in your business and enable you to become a success even faster. You can then duplicate these processes for your own success in business.

Once you get to a point in your business where you are successful and busy, the way to expand is to create a business for yourself that is more about how you work with other people. Duplicating yourself by bringing out the best in yourself and having other people come to work like you do can be an amazing way to take your business to the next level.

CHAPTER 33
YOUR CLIENT ON THE HERO'S JOURNEY

One of the quotes I love is from someone who I am extremely influenced by, and this is the work of the late Joseph Campbell. Joseph Campbell was a writer born in 1904. He passed away in 1987. The quote I most like from him is this. "We must be willing to get rid of the life we've planned so as to have the life that is waiting for us." In this chapter, I share with you some of the inspirations I have had from Joseph Campbell's work.

In 1949, Joseph Campbell wrote the book, "The Hero with a Thousand Faces." In this book he describes the way in which we go on our journeys in life. In 1990, the book "The Hero's Journey," a biography of Campbell's life was published. This book has influenced my understanding of human behaviour and this is manifested through my business.

When you unpack your business and unpack your understanding

of working with other people, where you stand is where you find your new potentials. I have found that things are not always what they seem, and yet there can be some patterns you will see in your business and in how you interact with other people that continue to manifest.

Understanding this in your clients can enable you to have an ultimate level of success you never thought imaginable. I like to find the extraordinary within ordinary. When I talk about ordinary, I talk about what is habitual, routine, and regular. What I look for is to find the remarkable and the very unusual, to go a logical level above, and to find ways to have an even higher meaning and higher success in everything that I do.

What I stand for is to step up to be remarkable in an existence that is habitual on Planet Earth. Why is this important? It helps you to avoid hit and miss. You can never worry about the reasons behind something when you're living at a higher level of logic. You can problem solve without becoming stressed and overwhelmed. The ability to operate at this level gives you connection with people like never before. It allows you to bring out the best in yourself and the best in others.

As a consequence, you can have even more confidence, happiness, and success. You'll have even greater skills in understanding other people, avoid conflict with ease, and problem solve without becoming overwhelmed. Most importantly, you can improve your skills in communication, which is something all leadership requires. I have found through working with people for many years is that there is a process involved you need to be aware of.

Once you have an understanding of where somebody is up to in their process, you can help and guide them to where they want to go. The most important thing I have found with the Hero's Journey is to never take it personally.

There is a system involved that enables people to achieve even more in their lives, and that system is never easy. In order for you to go to the next level, you have to be prepared to take the high road.

The high road is infinitely rewarding, and yet it is a process that involves you stepping out of the comfort zone of now in order to achieve what you want. When you have an understanding that every client and every person you work with is going to go through this process, your ability to help them and be of influence is quite profound. These themes are a part of the basic principles of evolution. The gradual development of something through stages of varying difficulty.

The Hero's Journey starts in the ordinary world. It starts with a call. It starts with a person wanting something and wanting to take their life in a new direction or to resolve something. Often it starts with a problem. Then the problem is ignored. This happens with your clients.

In Joseph Campbell's work he calls this refusing the call. I see this often in business. Someone will want some assistance with their business, and then they refuse the call. They sit back hoping it will all change, until one day when the issue is still unresolved they meet their mentor.

At this point they are about to cross the first threshold. They are about to get to that place where they can actually start to implement change. As you start to implement change, whether it's you or your client, you will find there are tests and temptations, trials, difficult times to go through. Your clients will start working with you and the changes they may need to implement in their life may not be easy. Results take effort.

As you shift and evolve, you need to be prepared to go through some trials and tribulations that will take you to the next level. These can sometimes be quite challenging, and it's time, then, to go within and realise you are in control and if it's to be, it's going to be up to you to make it happen.

What happens at this point is usually some kind of supreme ordeal, a crossing of the next threshold that allows you to go into extraordinary. This will always be a Hero's Journey. It's a rite of passage.

Once you've made a decision to go to this next level, you will find you get what is called boon. That is a time of accelerated progress in what you are doing. Your client experiences this when they are committed. Often you will see this with a client who has had a breakthrough in what you have been working with them on, and then all of a sudden everything starts to fall into place.

There are, of course, more things that need to be done in this process in order for that person to be able to achieve what they really want. Whether it's your client, or whether it's you, once you've gone through your supreme ordeal, you are on the road to influence. In your clients, this is the time they start referring business to you.

As you move into maturity, you become the observer. When you become the observer, you become the creator of your life. You will see this in your clients when they finally get to the point where they take true responsibility for their outcomes and they are able to manifest what it is they need for their own success. They then start sharing their success story and leading others.

You have been a part of this process, helping them go from the ordinary world in extraordinary ways. The next phase they will get to and you will get to is you will be a person of influence. This will give you the world at your feet.

The journey doesn't end there, because the world is still ordinary. Just around the corner will be your next calling. Your client will continue to have a process in their life that parallels the Hero's Journey, too. We all continue to go on this process as we evolve and develop.

Once you appreciate there is a process involved that unlocks potential like never before, you can look at it as a guiding force in how you can move forward in your life. This can be quite transformative. Experience the process knowing it is dynamic and moves. Absolve yourself from the stress of seeing a client go through the process when you now have the knowing it's perfectly designed for ultimate results.

A number of years ago I went to Italy. In Italy I looked at the Sistine Chapel and realised what I was looking at on the ceiling of a building was actually the Hero's Journey in action. It started off with an innocent frivolity, and then it moved into testing boundaries and taking a risk. As I walked through the building, I could see the next images were about accountability and consequences realised, about stepping up. Then I saw at the end there was mature influence.

Whether it's the process you take in your own business or the journey you take your client on, you will take them on a journey that involves a number of steps. These steps will involve innocence leading to a testing of boundaries and to new circumstances that enable somebody to step up.

Then they will lead to accountability and consequences. With that will come a major level of growth and out of that will come maturity and influence, and only then can the next journey begin.

In business, your task is to decode the system, to look behind what is happening, and to have a higher perspective by being the observer and creating what you want. Your ability to do this will be an enormous influence on your success and your position as a leader.

The best leaders I work with are people who are able to disassociate and look from the position of the outsider. They are able to dissolve emotional charge in situations and look at things from the point of view of creating what is required instead.

The steps to unlocking your potential start with looking at everything without judgment and just saying this could be or couldn't be, maybe or maybe not, and then being able to come from the position of influence by walking the high road and seeing what you could create.

When you are in situations where you work with other people and you appreciate the Hero's Journey, you will see that you need to check the emotional charge. Be alert to negative emotional behaviour in yourself, and be alert to negative emotional behaviour in others.

The only way to break the cycle is to be in observation, to look at what's going on, and then to create what you would like instead. You cannot change another person. You can only change yourself, and how you respond is very important.

When you appreciate that all processes involve a journey, you will be able to stay out of the drama and influence others by lifting them, because you have raised your conscious awareness.

You need to start by looking at the outside and then be honest about any secondary gain. What are you looking for? Is it attention, respect, appreciation, or love? Be honest, and find better ways to have what you really want and in this, you will find the secrets of true leadership on the Hero's Journey.

TRANSFORM YOUR SUCCESS EVEN MORE

"A leader is one who knows the way, goes the way and shows the way."
~ John C. Maxwell

Having a mentor by my side has been transformational in my life and I love to make a positive impact working with people just like you.

I would love you to join the vibration of Conscious Communication by visiting my website at www.madelainecohen.com and signing up for my FREE weekly Conscious Communication inspiration. You will hear from me every Monday morning with profound stories and ideas that you can use immediately to transform your own mindset, family, friends, colleagues and your community.

Mentoring

"When a leader lifts, everyone around them lifts too."

The work you do with me, has a ripple effect on everyone in your life. You will lead conscious communication within your family, relationships, businesses, and make an impact. Learning how you can make an impact rather than what you can get from a situation, will transform how you engage with the world.

In my working career I have delivered over $100M in sales to my clients and I thrive on helping people from what feels like a blank page. I have made a career of putting myself in situations that are seeming impossible – eg., like someone far removed from the boys sports club ending up in sports marketing negotiating multi-million dollar international deals; and a non-doctor owning one of the most successful healthcare practices in Australia.

All at the same time negotiating my way through 6 years of IVF to completing a complex divorce settlement in 3 months without a lawyer. We continue to work together and co-parent happy children who excel at school, music and sport.

The high road isn't easy, but at the same time it doesn't have to be a drama that feels like it is destroying your life. When you have the resources to make the complex into simple, you can get through it with grace and dignity.

I have walked the path before you, everything I share with you is possible, because I have done it!

How 1:1 Mentoring Works

- Your session starts with me from the moment you book, I will get a sense of you and determine the best strategy for our time together.

- I typically work with clients by phone and/or Skype, so you can be anywhere for these sessions; you could be in an airport lounge, in your car, out in the garden, in your living room. I don't want our mentoring to be an interruption in your life, I will fit each session around you.

- Sessions are for 1 hour, weekly or fortnightly, for 12 months. All sessions are recorded and I will send you this audio file at the end of each session.

- Payments are made by direct debit every month, so you don't need to spend the mental energy remembering to pay. Some of my clients have their sessions paid for by the company they work for.

These sessions can cover how to:

- Accelerate your career success

- Learn how to deal with drama

- Rise above workplace stress

- Learn what's behind the words people say

- Achieve holistic health outcomes

- Innovate and save time

- Become even more productive

- Create a life of balance

- Set and maintain healthy boundaries

- Take relationships to a higher level

- Find people who you resonate with

- Attract prosperity in your life

For more information and to complete an enquiry form go to www.madelainecohen.com or contact us on +61 2 9211 8153.

"Birds of a feather flock together. Energy is contagious. If you want to fly with the eagles, you'll have to stop swimming with the ducks."
~ from Secrets of the Millionaire Mind by T. Harv Eker

Contact Madelaine Cohen:

W: www.madelainecohen.com

E: madelaine@madelainecohen.com

P: + 61 2 9211 8153

L: www.linkedin.com/in/madelainecohen

ABOUT THE AUTHOR

Madelaine is a successful business leader and entrepreneur with a deep generosity in how she shares her most innovative communication strategies and "light bulb moment" experiences in leadership development, communications, marketing planning, commercialisation, sales, business and financial success. Her approach is entertaining and above all incredibly practical and life changing.

A businesswoman whose self-made success involves working with

Government based organisations and some of the largest companies in the world she has 25 years of experience as an entrepreneur, accredited training leader, mindset expert, speaker and mentor. Her leadership capability is expansive and she delivers results for senior executives and helps business owners. After "retiring" at the age of 21 to be an entrepreneur Madelaine has inspiring stories of hard work, immense personal and professional challenges, opportunities and success. As a business mentor she gets right to the point and compresses years and sometimes decades of learning into a session to create an immediate breakthrough.

In the early-1990's, Madelaine started her first business as a consumer products marketer including consulting for 15 years to Olympic, Commonwealth and Asian Games Committees. In this time, Madelaine's team delivered profitable and innovative multi-million dollar marketing programs to major sporting event organising committees globally. At the same time, she consulted and became the owner of a clinic in the healthcare industry.

Madelaine is the owner of Chirofamily Chirosports a well-loved Chiropractic clinic in Sydney's Eastern Suburbs which has been established for more than 20 years. She is probably one of the only non-practitioner owners of a highly successful independent healthcare practice in the Chiropractic industry in Australia. Her success in diverse business interests is attributed to her mindset, leadership and marketing skills. She is intuitive, a lateral thinker and reverse engineers business opportunities with formidable success. As a business mentor, Madelaine's experience and expertise transforms draining to amazing with step by step solutions and immediate results. She is an entertaining keynote speaker and a marketing and brand expert who mentors business people in the service sector who want to truly excel in professional development, communication excellence, influence, wealth creation and leadership.

www.ingramcontent.com/pod-product-compliance
Lightning Source LLC
Chambersburg PA
CBHW060556220326
41598CB00024B/3115